Ordinary people
doing extraordinary things

Mack Chrysler

Copyright (c) 2005 by Mack Chrysler
All rights reserved

KMC Publishing Company
Salt Lake City, Utah

ISBN: 0-9773364-0-9

DEDICATION

This book is dedicated to
the hundreds of selfless people
who have made *The Happy Factory* live -
and the thousands more who will make it last

The Happy Factory—Ordinary people doing extraordinary things

Table of Contents

Dedication

Prologue

Chapter 1 - An imperfect storm
How *Happy Factory* toys and Utah candy brightened Christmas 1998 for Honduran children in the wake of Hurricane Mitch

Chapter 2 - An unlikely beginning
Where and how Charles and Donna Cooley laid the foundations of *The Happy Factory*.

Chapter 3 - The turning point
Their factory-in-a-shed got a name, output and outlets broadened, and the Cooleys were stunned to learn how many needy children there are in the world.

Chapter 4 - The industrious elves of *The Happy Factory*
A typical day at the Cedar City, Utah, *Happy Factory* as 14 volunteers, busily glueing, clamping, tracing, sawing, drilling, sanding and branding, transformed hardwood scrap into toys.

Chapter 5 - Invaluable scrap
Remarkable new resources were tapped as word spread about the value the Cooleys and their volunteers were adding to donated wood.

Chapter 6 - A benevolent virus
The idea of taking wood that would be wasted and adding time that would be wasted to make toys to stimulate minds so they would not be wasted was so contagious that 25 more *Happy Factories* went into operation.

The Happy Factory—Ordinary people doing extraordinary things

Chapter 7 - A chain reacts
A local newspaper story about how *Happy Factory* toys were winning the hearts and minds of children in hospitals, Head Start centers, women's crisis centers, orphanages and other deserving places was picked up by the Associated Press national wire and opened all kinds of new windows on the world outside Cedar City.

Chapter 8 - Steam shovel therapy
Miniature hardwood *Happy Factory* steam shovels, with a bucket a child can fill and empty by manipulating two levers, proved to be therapy equipment in disguise for disabled children in the U.S. and abroad.

Chapter 9 - Uncommon helpers
The toy-making payoff is so personally satisfying that *Happy Factory* volunteers range from an ex-NBA basketball player and a barn builder to the Deputy Warden of a prison and a 'venture philanthropist.'

Chapter 10 - Going international
Toys speak a language of their own, understood by every child everywhere, witness the smiles generated by *Happy Factory* cars and trucks given away in Brazil, Bulgaria, China, Ghana, Liberia, Moldova, Paraguay, Romania, Tanzania, Vietnam and dozens of other countries.

Chapter 11 - What's next?
An energetic young Cedar City lawyer, elected President of *The Happy Factory* in 2004, the irreplaceable Cooleys and the Board of Trustees are now pondering how best to brighten the lives of even more needy children in the years to come.

Epilogue

The Happy Factory - Ordinary people doing extraordinary things

PROLOGUE

On November 9th, 2002, I had dinner at the Foreign Correspondents Club of Japan in Tokyo with an old friend, Boye Lafayette De Mente, author of 52 books.

We were on the 20th floor of the Denki Building, seated comfortably at a table in the Main Bar, ignoring the flashy neon lights of the Ginza district spread out below. Both of us had been living in the United States for many years and commuting regularly to Japan but had not seen each other for many months, so we had a lot of catching up to do.

Topics included not only comments about Japan's decline and fall into a 'lost decade plus' but my usual two questions: (1) how did he manage to survive and write his book, '<u>Once a Fool: From Tokyo to Alaska by Amphibious Jeep.</u>' a blow by blow account of a 4-month, 9,600 mile voyage in 1957 as crewman on the jeep, aptly named *Half Safe* with the owner, Australian Ben Carlin as skipper; and (2) what was he working on these days?

He laughed and explained that youth and plain dumb luck permitted successful completion of the amphibious adventure, with his relationship with Carlin the only major casualty. He then told me about the research he was doing for a new book on Japan. In turn, I filled him in about my current brain-picking among Japan's automotive experts, inside and outside of the auto-making companies, and added:

"It strikes me as ironic that as an automotive writer, 85th cousin of Walter P. Chrysler, founder of the Chrysler Corporation, I would end up making wooden cars."

That comment aroused his curiosity and I had to tell him about my stumble into toy making, little knowing where this confession would lead.

A couple of years before, my wife Sylvia and I had come across a heart-warming newspaper story about Charles and Donna Cooley in Cedar City, Utah. After retiring in 1995, the Cooleys had begun making wooden toys in a backyard shed. Once the needs of family, friends and neighbors had been filled, they began giving toys away to needy children. Before long, they formed *The Happy Factory*, a non-profit organization staffed by volunteers (in which no one, including the founders, was paid) and began producing toys on a full-time basis.

Since their cause was good and appealing, we sent them a modest contribution at Christmas to help cover expenses, and were put on the mailing list for their quarterly newsletter. Touched by the impact their simple toys were having on children who in many cases had never had one, I wrote Charles that summer to volunteer what help I might be able to offer, making parts or whatever in the shop I had in my garage. Charlie wrote back, suggesting I get in touch with Alton and Cheryl Thacker who were setting up *Happy Factory* #19 behind their house in Sandy, a Salt Lake City suburb.

As luck would have it, my get-acquainted appointment with the Thackers coincided with a drop-in visit by the Cooleys. Half an afternoon passed swiftly as Charles told stories about the tremendous difference a toy could make in the life of a child.

"It's amazing what happens when you hand a child a toy car or truck," he said. "First they run a finger across each wheel to make sure it turns. Next they stick a finger into the half inch hole we drill in them as a window. Then they play with it. In many cases, that toy is the first thing that child has ever owned. It gives the child a feeling of control, like a security blanket. It triggers their imagination and gives them something to love. Many take it to bed with them."

I told Boye that I was hooked. When Al Thacker's *Happy Factory* was completed that fall, I began spending a few hours each week living up to my namesake as a car maker, sawing, drilling, sanding and routing hardwood scrap into cars and trucks a few inches long that fit snugly into the hands of a deserving child.

Boye listened patiently and, when I finished my tale, said: "You've got a book there."

His suggestion caught me completely by surprise but the more I thought about it, the more I thought he was right. So did the Cooleys and their helpers, all of whom cooperated fully, and then some, in putting this book together. They were responsible for the story of *The Happy Factory*. I just fed the words into the computer. However, any mistakes in fact or interpretation are mine alone.

Mack Chrysler
Salt Lake City, Utah

The Happy Factory - Ordinary people doing extraordinary things

Chapter 1 - An imperfect storm

For several days in late October 1998, people in the tiny Central American republic of Honduras held their breath.

The warning signs were ominous. At 5 PM. Saturday, October 24th, a tropical storm with winds of 60 miles per hour was about 200 miles southwest of Kingston, Jamaica, and moving northward at about six miles per hour. Twenty-four hours later, the storm had become Hurricane Mitch with winds of 105 miles per hour, gusting to 120 miles per hour.

By 9 P.M. Monday, the hurricane's center was just west of Honduras' Swan Island and the residents of Honduras, one of the poorest countries in the Western Hemisphere, were resigned to another devastating blow from Mother Nature. Mitch had been upgraded to a Category 5 - the strongest hurricane going - with winds of 180 miles per hour, a force no one could adequately prepare for. Those along the coast began fleeing to higher ground. President Carlos Flores Facusse declared a state of maximum alert and sent Honduran Air Force planes to rescue the residents of outlying islands.

"Mitch is closing in, and God help us," said Mayor Monterrey Cardenas of Utila, an island twenty miles offshore.

Unfortunately, He didn't. On Tuesday, Hurricane Mitch struck the coast with vicious winds and heavy rain along a 350 mile wide front, ruining crops, drowning farm animals, swamping shanty towns and flooding some city streets to the tops of telephone poles. The toll in people and property steadily mounted.

"Mitch hit the Honduran coast last week and parked itself there, dumping several feet of rain onto the impoverished nation before moving across the Yucatan Peninsula and into the Gulf of Mexico. In Honduras, the largest cities have become virtual islands, accessible only by air," reported the Orlando [Florida] Sentinel on November 5th. "Overwhelmed by Hurricane Mitch's destruction and unable to provide Hondurans such basics as gasoline, food and water, the government made an urgent appeal for international aid."

In Cedar City, Utah, Charles and Donna Cooley were busily making wooden toys in the little *Happy Factory* shed behind their house. Like most people outside the storm zone, they were unaware of how bad things were in Honduras. Yet they were soon to provide a minor yet memorable part of the relief effort, although it was by no means easily managed.

Mitch, one of the deadliest hurricanes to hit the Western Hemisphere in two centuries, was so devastating that almost a week passed before the outside world became fully aware of the magnitude of the destruction - over 5,500 people killed and more than $4 billion in damages - and could respond. Among the first relief workers on the scene was a team from the Church of Jesus Christ of Latter-Day Saints (LDS), with food, medical supplies, clothing and other badly-needed staples of all kinds.

On November 21st, when LDS President Gordon Hinckley visited the capital city of Tegucigalpa for a first-hand look at how the relief effort was going, he embraced a little girl, the only survivor in her family, and said sadly that Honduran children probably wouldn't be getting any candy that coming Christmas.

His remark quickly got back to Salt Lake City and, within a day or two, several Utah candy companies had donated seven thousand pounds. The candy was flown to Honduras with other relief goods but Honduran Customs Officers held up the sweetest part of the shipment, ruling that candy was an unnecessary luxury in an extreme emergency and refusing it entry.

"Determining need is easier than delivering it," says William Reynolds, Manager of the church's Humanitarian Center in Salt Lake City.

The team of Mormon volunteers on the scene was disappointed but undeterred. After a brief huddle, the team leader asked innocently "Would Christmas presents be admitted?"

"Si," replied a perplexed senior Customs Officer. "Of course".

As quickly as he could get an international call through to Salt Lake City, the team leader telephoned the Humanitarian Center and asked for a hurry-up delivery of toys. There wasn't much time but an ample stock on hand included several hundred *Happy Factory* cars and trucks.

("When a disaster occurs, the time for preparation is past," says Garry Flake, Director of the LDS Humanitarian Emergency Services.)

When the little wooden vehicles and other toys arrived in Tegucigalpa, the Mormon volunteers took each toy, added some candy, and carefully wrapped the combined treats in colorful paper as a Christmas present, illustrating once again the old adage that 'there's more than one way to skin a cat' or, in this case, baffle a bureaucrat.

"We respond to disasters anywhere in the world," explains Flake, adding "Children are always silent observers when disasters hit. It's easy to forget them, easy to focus on food, shelter and clothing. Yet for a child, a toy is as life-giving and life-preserving as food. We need to do more for them."

The toys and the 'contraband candy,' probably the only bright part of Christmas that tragic year for most families in Honduras, established a new pattern. Since then, toys have been routinely added to emergency LDS relief shipments in response to earthquakes, floods, hurricanes, tornados and other natural disasters. This has reinforced the position of the Humanitarian Center as a major outlet for *Happy Factory* toys, abroad as well as at home.

"There's no commitment, no contract, no schedule, no pressure. We're just one of their outlets. They build toys and deliver what they can to us," explains LDS official Lloyd Pendleton

"The Cooleys worry every day about every needy child in the world and remind me of the old starfish story. The tide goes out, leaving starfish strewn along the beach. A little girl walks along, picking them up one by one and throwing them back in the water. A cynic asks her why she is attempting such a hopeless task. She ignores him, picks up a starfish, throws it back into the sea and says 'There's one more saved,'" says Flake.

In addition to Humanitarian Center shipments, *Happy Factory* toys are exported indirectly and directly by other Happy Factors such as Roland Anderson and Alton Thacker as well as the Cooleys. Like everything else that happened, there was nothing planned about these shipments. Top priority at *The Happy Factory* was - and is - satisfying local needs first. Yet boundaries have never been defined or imposed. When supply exceeded local demand or an unexpected need was identified, more *Happy Factory* toys began to hitchhike further and further away from home.

This movement has been ecumenical. Other religions and other organizations with needs regularly make requests for toys. All are fulfilled as a result of an unlikely success story that began several years ago in an unlikely place.

The Happy Factory - Ordinary people doing extraordinary things

Chapter 2 - An unlikely beginning

Cedar City, Utah, is the kind of small town you wish you'd been born and raised in, with friendly people, a beautiful setting and a pleasant climate. But it's by no means the usual small town. In fact, it began life as a fort and moved around a bit before settling down.

The first pioneers, dispatched 250 miles south from Salt Lake City by Mormon leader and prophet Brigham Young, arrived at Little Muddy Creek in late 1851 to fulfill one of his dreams by building an iron works. They spent that winter camped out in the boxes of their wagons, drawn up in a defensive circle. The following spring, for fear hostile Indians might fire down on them from a nearby hill, they moved their temporary fort to a new site a little further south and west of the hill, out of arrow range.

The prophet's project involved mining ore from a nearby deposit, building a blast furnace to produce pig iron, then shipping this crude iron to Salt Lake City to be manufactured into various products for sale in California. After five years of toil and trouble, however, with all shipments having to go by wagon train across some 1,000 miles of mountain and desert, the iron works finally floundered and had to be abandoned. The Mormon Church lost $600,000 in the venture, a considerable sum in those days.

Despite the inauspicious beginning, the Cedar City pioneers remained, taking care to move their fortified town to a third site when they found themselves living in the path of summer floods from the nearby southern Wasatch Mountains. Although ranchers continued to lose stock to Indian raids, sheep and cattle raising became the chief support of the community and the town stayed put, and small.

In later years, Cedar (as locals refer to it) became known for the nation's only asphalt golf course (mentioned in <u>Robert Ripley's Believe it or Not</u> some fifty years ago but long since gone), the Utah Summer Games, an award-winning annual Shakespearean Festival that attracts thousands of visitors each summer and fall and, most recently, *The Happy Factory*.

Says Cedar City Mayor Gerald R. Sherratt, "I've followed *The Happy Factory* from the shed stage. It represents the Cedar City spirit and has reflected well on our community of volunteers. Our Shakespearean Festival is all-volunteer and won a Tony Award [in 2001). Our Utah Summer Games, run by 2,000 volunteers, draw 30,000 people to the area every year. It is a unique project that pays off in self-satisfaction and it has generated the most publicity for Cedar since Ripley's report of what was actually a dirt golf course with asphalt 'greens' around the holes."

Despite the fiction and non-fiction, outsiders might still consider Cedar an unlikely place for an unlikely success story now gaining momentum nationally, year by year, as well as attracting more and more international attention. If so, they may be underrating that pioneer spirit which still prevails among many members of the community, including Charles and Donna Cooley.

They started out as simply and modestly as anyone could imagine with hand-made wooden lawn ornaments. This proved to be the beginning of a new adventure that no one, least of all the Cooleys, could have predicted. However, much went on before then to prepare the way, and some background helps identify the deep roots that underpin these descendants of sturdy pioneer stock and their *Happy Factory*.

Some of Charles' ancestors arrived in North America before the American Revolution. Originally from England, the Cooley family emigrated to Utah in 1850 from New York state. He was born in 1930 in Kaysville, Utah, a bit north of Salt Lake City, but raised in Cedar where his father taught woodworking in a branch of the Utah Agricultural College.

"Mine was a great child-hood.," says Charles. "I had one sister and two brothers and we all had chores to do. We had loving parents, enough to eat and never knew any hardship. I was as good a student as I wanted to be, and liked to play. The Christmas when I was four I got a red metal truck about four inches long that could go anywhere. One day it started up my mother's leg and reached her ankle before she squealed. I only did that once."

He adds that "I had pneumonia when I was five and had to learn to walk again which may have given me some empathy with deprived children."

Charles enlisted in the U.S. Air Force in December 1950 and served in Japan during the Korean War as a crypto operator with the Far East Material Command which was responsible for supplying the military with everything from ammunition to groceries. After his discharge in 1954, he spent a semester at Brigham Young University in Provo, Utah, which was memorable not for anything offered academically but because a friend introduced him to Donna Wilde.

She was born in 1935 and, like Charles, is descended from Mormon pioneers who include a great-grandfather, a convert from England, who joined a company of immigrants that pushed all their worldly possessions across much of the United States in two-wheel hand carts in 1856, and almost froze to death when stranded in Wyoming by an early winter blizzard.

The Wildes homesteaded in Summit County east of Salt Lake City where Donna grew up.

She says: "My father was a farmer and cheese maker. I had one brother and two sisters and our family struggled like all farm families did in Oakley Valley. My folks really taught us how to work. I only had three dolls in my life and I still have one of them."

Donna relates to 'disadvantaged children' in a personal way, explaining that "I was born with bad hearing and my playmates made fun of me, which was hurtful. My parents were told I would have to attend a school for the deaf and dumb. However, by age four, I'd had two mastoid operations which improved my hearing enough to let me attend regular schools."

Donna and Charles were married in 1955, the year Charles completed his studies at Southern Utah University (SUU), the successor to the Utah Agricultural College, after working his way through school as a night clerk at the Escalante Hotel in Cedar. He graduated with a degree in Business Administration, a major he describes as "the easiest one there was," and they settled down in Cedar where she worked in a local bank and he began selling farm implements.. Two years later, daughter Jolene was born, followed by daughter Kristine in 1959.

The next year, a third 'member' was added to the family when Charles became the only man (or boy) in Cedar City with his own, full-size fire engine. He'd driven through Mesquite, Nevada, shortly after the town fathers replaced their 1923 Seagrave with a new fire engine and the old one was parked outside the firehouse For Sale. The price was right - about $200 - so be bought it.

He and a buddy hitched his new 1960 Ford 4WD pickup

to the Seagrave and began the 90 mile haul north to Cedar. Unfortunately, the hitch was tight and the heavy-steering Seagrave tended to veer, lifting the rear end of the pickup sharply to right and left on every veer, but somehow they made it home unscathed.

The care and feeding of a fire truck with a 50 gallon fuel tank and 30 gallon oil tank was unexpectedly expensive, so it was not driven much but Charles was behind the wheel one day when the Cedar City volunteer fire department passed him with sirens wailing and bells ringing. Naturally he gave chase to the fire, his first and last in his personal fire truck. The flames were soon dampened and so was Charlie as the firemen turned their hoses on him and the uninvited Seagrave. To his regret, it finally became a burden and was abandoned. Donna, however, did not shed a tear over their loss.

In 1962, the local sheriff requested help for his ten deputy force, spread too thinly around too much territory. Charles, his friend Alan Garfield and ten other volunteers were deputized as the founding members of the Iron County Civil Defense Auxiliary (CDA) police, less formally referred to as the "jeep patrol." They furnished their own guns, ammunition and vehicles and, since he was the only member with a four wheel drive vehicle, Charles was named Commander. They were on call 24 hours a day, seven days a week, and did whatever was needed, from crowd control to finding lost hunters and locating a downed aircraft in a swamp.

"We had a lot of fun," says Garfield, justifiably proud that the CDA eventually became a Search and Rescue unit still operating in the county today.

But they all had to earn a living as well. Charles was a born salesman, with the instincts of an entrepreneur, and his regular job was selling. Farm equipment was followed by fire and casualty insurance and auto parts, in Utah and

Nevada. In 1970, he started Alpine Pest Control Company in Cedar, the first of its kind in Iron County, and ran a carpet cleaning business on the side to generate more income. Nine years later, impressed by a <u>60 Minutes</u> television report on commercial solar heating units, he telephoned Piper Hydro Inc., in Anaheim, California, and secured the first franchise in Utah. Alpine Pest Control was sold, Utah Solar Corporation was formed and all went well for four years until 1983. Interest rates soared, construction virtually stopped, several million dollars worth of contracts evaporated and the business went bust. There wasn't much call for carpet cleaning, either, and Charles was dismayed to find that, at age 53, he could not compete in the job market without computer knowledge and subsequently was unemployed for 19 months. Fortunately, Donna had left the bank in 1970 to become Secretary to Ken Benson, Dean of Students at SUU, and was promoted to Head Cashier two years later, a position she held until she retired.

With Donna Cooley in charge of the money, State auditors said SUU had the fewest bad checks of any university in Utah. They noted that, while bad checks in a typical year at a typical university or college in Utah might reach $20,000, they totaled only a few hundred dollars at SUU because Donna telephoned the deadbeats and insisted they pay up.*

* (Footnote - The Cooley marriage, like so many, united two opposites. As Charles explains, "Donna goes to any length to get the job done right while I take the course of least resistance.")

When a job as custodian opened up at the university in 1985, Charles was quick to apply. He says "It was the best selling job I ever did. I told the people at SUU that I was the greatest custodian in the world and they believed me."

Evidently his deeds matched his words and the following May he began managing the university's new Centrum, a 5,400 seat special events center in operation twelve months a year, handling everything from basketball games and ballet to performances by symphony orchestras and the Mormon Tabernacle Choir.

"Charlie did a great job managing the Centrum with the SWAT team he formed. Those initials stood for Sweat, Work and Tears," says his friend Garfield, referring to the team of students employed to keep the Centrum spic and span.

Whenever they could escape job pressures and stress, the Cooleys welcomed the chance to recharge their batteries in the cabin they built in 1960 on a twenty acre piece of the 6,000 acre ranch of Charles' boyhood friend, Ed Larsen, in the Wasatch foothills twenty-six miles east of Cedar. It was a two bedroom and sleeping loft, Do-It-Yourself project, and construction was relatively easy.

Says Charles "I've always been handy around the house and I've been exposed to wood all my life, with my father a wood-working teacher and my brother Frank a master cabinet maker and home builder."

Still, to be on the safe side, he enlisted Frank to cut the angled trusses for the roof. And Donna, who is no slouch with a saw or hammer, is quick to remind him that "We built that cabin *together*."

Says daughter Kristine: "We spent weekends all summer long in the cabin and it became a huge part of our lives, supplying the most family time. We helped tend Larsen's sheep and played games at night and Dad didn't let us win at hard games like pinochle, euchre and hearts. Mom and Dad both worked and we all had chores. When they got into the carpet cleaning business, Jolene and I were paid by the hour, at the regular rate. We signed in and out and had a wage book."

Adds daughter Jolene Cooley Lee: "Our parents taught us the value of hard work, and Kristine and I made good money working in their carpet cleaning business. We were paid the same as a hired man and we did a man's work. We learned honesty and integrity and, when I won a hand of euchre, I felt so good. Dad was a good salesman. One year, he sold more Monroe shock absorbers than anyone in Nevada and we got almost everything in the catalog of prizes - sleeping bags, electric tools, bedspreads, sets of dishes. It was like Christmas when the prizes arrived."

Jolene likens her father to an inventor. "Nothing he does surprises me. I went to him once and said Eric [her son] should have a fort. Everything Dad does starts on grid paper and, before he was done, Eric's fort was built on poles four feet off the ground and had a retractable ladder and a flagpole with 'Lee' on it. We christened it Fort Lee."

Says Kristine: "Dad was always supportive with my last minute school projects like the Pioneer project in 7th Grade. He could make anything."

In 1985, Kristine began teaching kindergarten in Enoch Elementary School and soon asked Charles to make toys for the kids.. Her first request was for him to make a train big enough for her kids to get on and into.

"Do you have plans?" he asked.

"No," she replied.

He went ahead anyway, got some plywood and constructed a kid-size train 3 feet wide, 6 feet long and 3 feet high. Master cabinet maker Frank, never impressed by his brother's amateur woodworking ability, stopped by one day when the train was parked in the carport of the Cooley's Cedar City house being painted.

"Who built the train?" Frank asked suspiciously.

"Kris' kindergarten class," Charles replied with a straight face.

His elder brother found this reasonable and replied with a nod "They did a pretty good job."

Donna apparently wasn't all that impressed either. In 1989, when they bought 2 ½ acres of land with a mobile home on it some eight miles west of Cedar, he told her he wanted to add a small shop and she said "Why? You never made anything."

But, always an understanding wife, she didn't object when Charles hammered together a 10 foot by 20 foot shed behind their new house. The next year, he purchased a scroll saw and sander, bought some twisted boards at a lumber yard because they were cheaper than the straight ones and cut out a half dozen wooden ornaments to decorate their yard which had been left as bare dirt after the removal of all the kosher weed. Donna joined in the re-decoration by giving the ornaments a colorful coat of paint.

Removing the weeds had been the job of twin goats, a gift from friends. Itch and Scratch, so named by Charles, initially practiced on Donna's flower bed. They escaped repeatedly from a fenced pasture and eventually bent the fencing on their way out before eating flowers, weeds and everything else they came across.

The Cooleys decided the goats had to go but, to their dismay, no one was interested. Finally Charles took them to auctioneer Bret Whittier who told him what he already knew, namely that there wasn't much demand for goats, and that he'd be lucky if they brought $15 each.

Charles was out of town the day of the auction but checked the next morning with Bret who said "You're not going to believe this."

Charles sighed, expecting to hear his goats had not sold, and was shocked to receive a check for $187. It seems the auctioneer had opened the sale by saying "We've got a real treat for you today, a pair of goats. Itch and Scratch." The bidding promptly took off and kept going up and up. A man who raised thoroughbred horses finally got both goats, paying mainly for the names, but also because the presence of goats, for some reason, has a calming effect on high-strung horses.

  Neither the goats nor the lawn ornaments held much attraction for daughter Kris who had more ambitious projects in mind for her students and her father's spare time. The train was just a start. In 1986, he built her kindergarten class a helicopter. The next year he constructed a castle, complete with battlements and a gate the kids could walk through. A ship was next in 1988 and a log cabin arrived in 1989. Before she - and he - were done, people had begun asking "What's your Dad going to make this year?"

  Donna confesses wryly, "Neither one of us could ever say 'No' to our daughters."

  The ship, 5 feet 6 inches wide by 5 feet high by 12 feet long, was too wide to fit through the three foot classroom door. Charles had to cut it in half, lengthwise, for re-assembly in her classroom. When the principal of Kris' school stopped by to inspect the newest addition, he was puzzled. He couldn't figure out how anything so big could suddenly appear in his school.

  "My father had to put it in a bottle to get it inside," explained Kris without a smile.

  Her students, like most kids, took small miracles for granted and accepted the new addition without question and with considerable enthusiasm.

  "That ship has been all over the world, wherever a child's imagination could take it," says Charles who designed it with a bridge above and Captain's Quarters below, both of which Kris uses as a reward. Her pupils

The Happy Factory

take turns each day wearing the Captain's cap, standing on the bridge and sitting in the Quarters - provided they've done their homework.

Says Charles: "Kris prepared me for *The Happy Factory*. I'd always been creative, dating back to my childhood. If we wanted something, we had to make it - floats out of match boxes for the Fourth of July and so on. Our kids liked what I made later but what amazed me is what Kris did with the things I made for her kindergarten class."

By June 1995, when both Cooleys retired from SUU, that kindergarten classroom was stuffed with Charles' creations. A new workshop 22 feet by 26 feet had risen beside the shed, a band saw had been added to the tool collection and the lawn ornaments had long ago been succeeded by the 34 small mother-baby animal sets in The Winfield Collection, which offered woodcraft patterns and supplies for sale by mail. Each part of these layered sets was carefully sawn out by Charles and painted by Donna.

As they got a little better at it, Donna says "We thought we might be able to make toys and sell them."

That July, they attended the Washington County Fair "on the hottest day of the hottest month in the hottest part of Utah," says Charles. There they found stall after stall of poorly-made wooden toys of various kinds on sale for fifty cents and a dollar each. It was a discouraging eye-opener that indicated toy-making as a business might neither be rewarding nor satisfying.

Earlier that year, however, they had been approached by Peg Whetten, a friend of 20 years and the wife and assistant of an orthodontist who divides his practice between Cedar and Las Vegas. Whetten was so taken by the animal sets they produced with such loving care that she suggested taking some to the craft show she and two friends held each year in one of their homes in Las Vegas.

Their 'A Touch of Class' two-day shows in mid-September, were by invitation only and aimed at new home buyers with children. Quality items were featured, and Peg considered *The Happy Factory* animals would be a perfect fit.

"You make them, I'll sell them," she promised.

The Cooleys spent most of their spare time making 300 of the animal sets which Peg duly hauled to the craft show. Half of them sold for around $10 a set and Charles spent some of the proceeds on a 10-inch Sear's table saw. ("Anything to make him happy," said Donna.)

Donna was President of the Relief Society of the Church of Jesus Christ of Latter-Day Saints' Stake in Cedar that year and, in October, planned a trip to check on the needs of the Primary Children's Medical Center (PCMC) in Salt Lake City for the quilts the Relief Society ladies made. Charles decided to tag along for the ride and put five boxes of toys, left over from the Las Vegas 'invitational,' in the trunk of their car on the off chance patients might like them.

Patients at Primary Children's, ranging from newborns to 21-year-olds, were treated for 40 different medical problems including birth defects, cancer, cystic fibrosis, diabetes, epilepsy and spina bifida. The 232-bed facility served five states in the inter-mountain West and welcomed gift-in-kind donations such as quilts, clothes and toys that expand the 'tender, loving care' side of the hospital's operation.

"There is so much more we can do for a child with things our budget does not cover," explained Marie Hendriksen, an administrator in the PCMC Foundation office.

"These include giving small rewards to a child under stress - for enduring an invasive procedure such as drawing blood or having to drink barium prior to having an X Ray taken or being immobilized with straps for medical imaging," she said. "Patients earn 'points' toward rewards as well for doing things that the physically able take for granted - simple exercises that rehabilitation specialists request such as standing up, stretching a leg or bending an arm."

On arriving at the Medical Center, Donna had no trouble getting the quilt sizes and guidelines she needed from a helpful lady at the Front Desk, after which the Cooleys were directed to a meeting on the fourth floor with Ms. Hendriksen. Somewhat diffidently, Charles opened the box of animal sets he'd lugged into the conference room where they met, and spread some of them out on the table. He was pleasantly surprised by her reaction.

Said Hendriksen: "I was touched and over-whelmed and the Cooleys were amazed that the things they'd made were needed and wanted."

Hendriksen was so pleased with the unexpected gifts, and so delighted with the offer of four additional boxes that, when she met the Cooleys in the parking lot with a cart, she had tears in her eyes and said to them "Just a minute. I have to have a hug."

Charles later said "We get more hugs at Primary Children's Medical Center than we do at a family reunion."

The Happy Factory - Ordinary people doing extraordinary things

Chapter 3 - The turning point

The first trip to Primary Children's Medical Center (PCMC) in Salt Lake City was a pivotal turning point in Charles and Donna Cooley's new career as toy makers and givers.

Marie Hendriksen was familiar with the different needs of her colleagues at the Medical Center and took care to show the animal sets to staffers in Rehab/Neuro Science, Medical Imaging, Child Life (specializing in educating, entertaining and helping a child cope with his/her medical condition) and other departments.

Within a week, the five boxes were empty and the 150 toys in the initial delivery had been distributed. Within a month, all the toys were in the hands of delighted patients as 'rewards.' And Charles Cooley must have been psychic. Almost exactly a month after the first delivery was made, he telephoned Marie.

"Could you use more toys?" he asked.

Could she ever! Although they weren't soft or cuddly, the Cooley toys were unusual, special and treasured. Before long, they were delivering wooden "flippers," lawnmowers, pull-toys, helicopters and assorted other toys as well as the layered animal sets. Here are some of the things that happened, as told to Donna Cooley.

* A physically and mentally abused 9 year old girl, too frightened to speak after admission to the Medical Center, kept looking at the animal sets on a shelf behind a therapist. Asked if she would like one, she responded by nodding up and down and pointed to a mother panda bear and its baby. After holding them tightly for a few minutes, she began responding to the therapist's questions and could be helped.

* A 14 year old girl with terminal cancer felt she had little to live for. She was moody and cranky and would not visit with

the other children. Shortly before Christmas, a nurse offered her a Cooley toy and she picked the mother giraffe and baby, with bow ribbons around their necks. It was love at first sight and she took them to bed with her. On Christmas morning, when the nurse checked in on her, she had placed her wooden giraffes under the small Christmas tree by her bed.

* After a young boy came out of surgery, the first thing he asked for when the anesthetic wore off was his mother lion and baby set.

* Some toys unexpectedly had therapeutic value. A five year old boy was admitted to the hospital after suffering a stroke. It is unusual for such a young child to have a stroke and he could not understand why he couldn't use his left arm and hand. After considerable rehabilitation, Child Life specialists gave him a "flipper" and were as delighted as their patient when he forced himself to work it with his left hand as well as his right. The "flipper" went home with him to help speed his recovery.

In a letter of thanks, Sharon Goodrich, Director of Annual and Corporate Giving, wrote "We feel like it's Christmas every time the Cooleys come to visit! Those of us who are privileged to work at Primary Children's know well that the best medicine doesn't always come from a bottle. Sometimes it is a toy or a game that seems to make the hurt go away."

On one of their delivery trips to the Medical Center, Charles gave a Hocus Pocus stick to Child Life specialist Tony Smith and showed him how it worked. On the next trip, as they were unloading toys, Smith came running into the room.

"I've got to tell you about the Hocus Pocus stick!" he said.

Smith had been working with a little boy with a terrible disease that short-circuited his brain and prevented him from functioning normally physically. The disorder is treatable but motor skills must be re-learned and the biggest problem with children is depression. He had given the boy the Hocus Pocus stick and showed him how it worked.

"You can't believe the progress he's made in the last two weeks," Smith said. "The therapists who come in each morning to work with him want to know how it works but he won't show them. He thinks he's about the biggest man in the hospital. Isn't it interesting that we have equipment in this hospital worth millions of dollars and this simple twenty cent wooden stick did the trick?"

These stories were typical of the payback the Cooleys enjoyed. They had begun toy-making to satisfy themselves. Says Donna: "Most people just didn't understand that we were making toys for children because we wanted to, not for pay or anything else. We had no wish to attract attention and, when asked what we were doing, Charles would reply with a grin 'just making sawdust.'"

The positive reaction to their toys at Primary Children's changed their perspective on the importance of what was taking place in the little shop behind their home.

"Our reception there gave us a reason to make toys and now we had an outlet," says Charles.

Donna adds "Carole Woodside, PCMC Foundation Manager, said 'You're being selfish by keeping your toy-making activities quiet. Don't you know charity is contagious?' Then people in Cedar began quizzing us and asking to help with the painting so the secrecy kind of exploded.. The best way to get the word out is to try to keep something a secret."

What began as a private hobby was turning into a full-time labor of love, absorbing most of the Cooley's days and nights and most of their spare cash as well, now that more and more wood and paint were needed to match the increase in output. Early in 1996, their friend Paul Cozzens, owner of Cozzens Cabinets in Cedar, took Charles to see Mark Messer at Timberline Cabinet Doors. That visit solved one problem and created another.

Messer was so impressed by the toy makers' aims that he agreed to set aside scrap for them from his door-making operation. This changed the supply of wood from the crooked pine boards the Cooleys had been buying from a lumber yard because they were cheap to a mix of hard-wood board ends and strips that were free-for-the-taking.

But the 7/8" x 2 ½" strips were too small for the Winfield Collection three-layered animal sets which averaged around 3" x 5" for the mothers and 1 ½" x 2" for the babies. So, initially,

Charles burned them in the wood stove he used to heat the shop. However, a few weeks later, he arrived on a wood run after Timberline had just finished house-cleaning their shop and ended up with a whole pickup load of strips.

Says Charles: "I knew I couldn't burn all that wonderful hardwood and wondered what to do with it. While driving home, a little light went on in my mind and I said to myself, 'Hey, stupid, why don't you make the patterns fit the wood instead of vice-versa?'"

Back at the shop, he sat down with grid paper and a pencil and drew the patterns for several little vehicles - a sedan, land rover, bug, jeep and truck - that are still being made today. Their size was strictly dictated by the strips - no more than two and a half inches high, only seven-eighths of an inch thick.

However, after cutting them out on the band saw, he felt they were "kinda thin" and decided to experiment by gluing two of the strips together. This doubled the width and produced far better proportions. The designs were inspired, not only a perfect fit for Cooley's simple woodworking tools but for the hands of little children as well. He knew hardwood toys were superior to those made of softwood.

He explains with a grin "When little children get their first teeth, they're like beavers."

Charles was concerned that his 'clients' at Primary Children's might not find the vehicles acceptable and was relieved to learn there was no need to worry on that score. By then, hardly six months after the first delivery, Cooley toys had already become unofficial but important 'medicine' at the hospital. The little vehicles were welcomed with open hands, large and small, not only at the Medical Center but at a new outlet only a few blocks away.

Close by was Shriners Hospitals for Children Intermountain, a 40 bed hospital with three full-time surgeons on staff, one of 19 Shriner's hospitals in North America specializing in orthopaedic treatment of children with problems of the bones, muscles, ligaments and joints. Admission is based on need and treatment is free. The bright and cheerful facility in Salt Lake City treats over 4,000 children each year, both out-patients and in-patients, from surrounding states and the Juarez area of Mexico.

The Cooleys had heard good things about Shriners and arrived there on the morning of May 1st, 1996, unannounced, with a variety of toys. They were escorted to a second floor office holding many toys and were met by Kristi Kyte, a therapist. She examined the toys they'd brought and said enthusiastically "I'd definitely like to have some of these."

A couple of dozen toys were left with her and three more deliveries were made before the year was out. Included in the mix were layered animal sets, flippers, a hippopotamus on wheels and other pull-toys, wooden rabbits, whales, frogs and a brontosaurus.

The response of Shriner's patients was every bit as positive as those experienced a few blocks away in the Medical Center. And there were poignant tales to be told as well, two of which starred the flippers.

* A Shriners secretary concluded the flipper could work miracles, explaining that one morning she passed a room in which a young girl was screaming with pain but could not have any more pain medicine for a while. When handed a flipper and shown how it worked, the child quit crying and began playing with it, her pain temporarily forgotten, until it was medication time again.

* Surgery to both legs left a 10 year old boy in a cast from his toes to his knees. Constant pain made him hard to handle and naughty, given to misbehavior like pulling out his IVs, until he was given a flipper. The boy's father didn't know - or care - whether his son liked the toy or whether it made him angry because he couldn't get it to work the way he wanted it to. What mattered most was the flipper kept his son's mind off his pain and too preoccupied to give the nurses and doctors trouble.

However, Charles explains that "We found the two hospitals were two entirely different operations. Primary Children's had far more patients, a greater turn-over, and a need for more little toys. Shriners was much smaller and specialized with children who have bone, muscle and joint problems."

Consequently, the Cooleys took a different tack at the Shriners Hospital. With sufficient funds available to purchase regular toys, staffers there felt other organizations with tighter budgets should get the free toys offered by *The Happy Factory*. They preferred to use the Cooleys as a special resource, to make things they could not easily find elsewhere.

Lisa Carter, a physical therapist, explained that "We had unique needs and I was always looking for resources. When I called Charles and asked if he could make us wedge boards that assist children to stretch and strengthen tight or weak muscles, he said 'Sure, just send us the plans.'"

Subsequently, Charles' and Donna's trips to Shriners were principally to deliver special orders for simple equipment which was either unavailable or unaffordable commercially. These included a transfer board that allowed a child with muscular dystrophy to be moved from his wheelchair to his bed without his mother having to physically lift him, a wooden tray/easel combination that allowed a 16 year old girl confined to a wheelchair with cerebral palsy and spastic paralysis to write without the pain of bending forward.

Says Lisa Carter "The Cooleys never said 'No.'"

In addition to catering to the Shriners Hospital's special needs, Charles and Donna continued supplying toys to Primary Children's. In 1995 and 1996, they made eleven trips from Cedar to Salt Lake City and delivered over 800 toys, each branded 'By Cooley.' On one of those trips to the Medical Center, they were surprised to be told that "Although none of our patients and parents know who you are, so many kids now have toys 'By Cooley' that you're famous."

That stuck in Charles' mind.

A few weeks later, on a chilly morning in November 1996 when Donna was doing laundry and he was standing in front of the east window in the shop, cutting out more toys, an interesting idea popped into Charles' head. It was possibly triggered by the smiling faces of the children at Primary Children's and Shriners as they clutched their precious hardwood toys - who can ever know for sure exactly where inspiration comes from? At any rate, he pondered and sawed and pondered a while longer. The idea kept coming back, louder and clearer, until he finally turned off the saw and walked into the house.

"What do you think about *The Happy Factory*?" he asked Donna.

"That's cute. What is it?" she responded.

"That's us," he said.

"Oh, I like that."

They soon found out *The Happy Factory* was a magic name that underscored what they were doing, attracted favorable attention and opened doors (and, eventually, a building as well.) In the meantime, Charles continued to minimize his woodworking ability even though it was becoming formidable.

"I saw a picture of a rocking horse in the Winfield Collection and wanted to make one," he explains. "I had no use for a rocking horse so, when it was finished, I gave it to Primary Children's." He adds that "as I got better equipment and became more skillful, I changed my approach. In the beginning, for example, I favored the quickest way to get things done and didn't rout the edges of the toys. Then I decided to take more time with fit and finish and quality improved."

So did the scope of Charles' woodworking ambition. In February 1997, after two years spent considering the problems involved in making anything so complicated, he dusted off plans for a 1/10th scale Conestoga wagon drawn by four scaled-down oxen and began sawing, carving, bending and gluing the 200 parts. The four spoke wheels were an unexpected challenge. So were the oxen. But seven weeks later, they were hitched properly to the wagon, the demanding project was completed and eventually found a permanent home prominently displayed in the Daughters of the Utah Pioneers Museum in Cedar.

But the Conestoga project was only a side issue. Toys were the main event and the animal sets and little cars and trucks were followed by a miscellany of other wooden toys from *The Happy Factory*, including tractor trailers, flat bed trucks, helicopters, flippers, pull toys, puzzle boards, Hocus Pocus sticks, Whatzits and miniature steam shovels on which a child could sit and work the levers (more about them later.)

   The Happy Factory was busy filling special requests as well. Out of the little shop came several lapboards used in Primary Children's Pediatric Intensive Care Unit as tables to put on beds, two Rocking Horses, a Rocking Airplane and a mini Rat-tail Rocking Hardly Davidson motorcycle (a special favorite of the boys), a four door box Buckboard Bench, a large Irish mail car, a brontosaurus, lawnmower and five little red wagons. The wagons, complete with side rails, were padded with quilts so the children could ride in comfort as parents pulled them around the Medical Center hallways. When ready to go home, most insisted on making the trip to their parent's car in a red wagon rather than a wheelchair.

   Recalls Tony Smith: "I remember requesting several items for blind patients and Charles made different texture boards and games that blind patients could use. He saved us hundreds of dollars by making items simply from looking at a picture of them in a catalog. We still have them on the unit and still use them. Of everything the Cooleys donated, the flipping clowns went first and fast and were always popular with the children for Bingo prizes. They were all hand-painted with detailed designs, as were most of the Cooley toys."

   Smith asked to have some of the animal sets delivered in pieces, unglued and unpainted, so the children could assemble and paint them in what proved to be a helpful therapeutic exercise. The 'toy therapy' took other forms as well.

   He says "One patient had cerebral palsy and, although a teenager, was delayed to about the age of a toddler or preschooler. He would sit sometimes for 30 or 40 minutes making his clown flip and flop. Although I can't remember many specific stories, I do know that the hundreds and hundreds of toys the Cooleys donated to the hospital made a difference. Many children gained joy and pleasure from their toys. And many parents were grateful for the small simple gift a toy brought to their child in a hospital where uncertainty and often physical discomfort can make it very difficult for children."

Tests at the Medical Center on Susie, a 13-year old girl, indicated she had multiple sclerosis and ,as if that wasn't cruel enough, was destined to go blind as well. In the radiological department were three shelves of *Happy Factory* toys including a variety of animal sets that reminded Susie of Noah's Ark. Her mother Barbara asked the staff who made the toys and telephoned the Cooleys to ask if she could buy some of the animal sets. Donna explained that, as a non-profit charitable organization, *The Happy Factory* couldn't sell toys but would give her some. She talked it over with Charles and they decided to make an exotic wood Nativity scene as well.

As Donna tells the story: "What a wonderful experience it was meeting Susie. She was a bright and beautiful young lady and was thrilled when we entered her room with the toys and the Nativity scene. We sensed her feelings. She and her mother were grateful and Barbara said Susie will be able to feel the shape of the toys after she goes blind. Barbara hugged us and we shed some tears together as we left the hospital. Experiences like this make it all worthwhile."

Another rewarding experience involved Jacob, the two year old grandson of friends in Cedar who was gravely ill at Primary Children's. He had been transferred from intensive care to Rehab when the Cooleys arrived with *Happy Factory* toys painted for him by his aunt. When the tractor/trailer, bus and puzzle were laid on his bed, the little boy reached for them and his mother said that was the first sign of encouragement she had seen. She added that he liked trucks and knew the names of them but would not talk. Three weeks later, Donna called Jacob's mother and learned that he was walking, starting to talk, and loved his diesel tractor/trailer. She felt the toys marked the start of his recovery.

Says Donna "You cannot tell us these toys don't work."

Marie Hendriksen is a meticulous book-keeper and reports that, in the five years from 1995 to the year 2000, the main *Happy Factory* outlet was Primary Children's Medical Center. In that period, a remarkable 5,426 toys were delivered. The estimated the value of these gifts was $81,141.

Nor was the taste for *Happy Factory* toys limited to the

Medical Center and Shriners, as the Cooleys discovered when they made their first visit to the Humanitarian Center in Salt Lake City. At that time, it was still called the Sort Center, established by the Church of Jesus Christ of Latter-Day Saints (LDS) in 1991, six years before, and housed - ironically - in a building constructed by Remington Small Arms to manufacture bullets and bombs during World War II.

The plain-Jane Sort Center name came naturally enough from its function. Only 15% of the clothes donated to the church-owned Deseret Industries (DI) retail stores sell. After three weeks, unsold clothing was - and is - shipped in DI trucks to the Humanitarian Center. Each year around 20 million pounds of used clothing arrives in 700 and 800 pound bales and is sorted into eight categories for quality and usability. The not-so-good is sold for rags and the good is cleaned, repackaged in 100 pound bundles and shipped to the needy.

Clothing is still the first priority of the Humanitarian Center but operations have expanded to include medical supplies and equipment, school kits, hygiene kits, new born baby kits, quilts and toys. Some 4,000 hand-made quilts arrive each month. Used seat covers donated by Delta Airlines are converted into balls and attractive bags for the school and hygiene kits. And *The Happy Factory* has become an important source of toys.

Donna had been promising herself a call on the Sort Center to see if any of the Relief Society projects such as quilts, hygiene kits and school kits might be useful so, early one morning in October 1997, she and Charles arrived unannounced. They were given a tour and saw circles of volunteers busily sorting the good from the bad, forklift trucks moving bales of clothes, a collection of refurnished medical equipment awaiting shipment and piles of books to be included in school kits.

When he spied a wooden toy on a counter, Charles asked their host, Robert Workman, if the Sort Center could use toys.

"Oh my, yes," said Workman. "Do you realize there are five hundred million children in the world without a toy?"

That shocking statistic made Charles feel inadequate. He explained that "At *The Happy Factory* we make wooden toys but we couldn't make a drop in the bucket for a need like that."

Workman politely disagreed. "One toy may only be a drop in the bucket of the world's needs but it's a big drop for the child who gets it."

The next month the Cooleys made their first delivery of toys to the Sort Center, and regular visits followed. The next spring, Lloyd Pendleton, the Sort Center Manager, thanked them personally for what they were doing and urged them to take care of their local needs first and bring any surplus to Salt Lake City.

Charles was surprised. "But we don't have any local needs."

"You might want to look around. Check with your hospitals and crisis centers," said Pendleton.

Back home they did as he suggested and found that places like the Canyon Creek Women's Crisis Center and Head Start for pre-schoolers could use the toys they made.

"Word of mouth reports soon began to pass around and we discovered all kinds of local needs. In fact, for a while we didn't think we'd have a surplus for the hospitals and Sort Center in Salt Lake City but more volunteers showed up, production increased and supplies met demand," explains Charles. "That was a most beautiful meeting. Lloyd gave us confidence in what we were doing. He was the first person we met who impressed on us the importance toys have for children."

Coordination between the Humanitarian Center and *The Happy Factory* was relaxed. As mentioned earlier, Pendleton saw no need for a contract or commitment or schedule but was happy to have the Cooleys deliver whatever toys they could.

A year later, at his suggestion, the Cooleys photographed each toy they were making. These photographs were reproduced in a catalog that was sent as an order book to 54 humanitarian missionaries serving abroad. Before ordering, they were instructed to have local children indicate which toys they would most like to have. Out of the 21 toys illustrated in the catalog, only nine were the first choice of the children - the Bug, Bus, Land Rover, Jeep, Milk truck, Sedan, Truck, helicopter and elephant.

"We'd been making all kinds of toys which appealed mostly to adults. What was important was finding out what kids liked most," says Charles. From then on, most *Happy Factory* production has consisted of these small cars and trucks, and the Humanitarian Center has remained a major outlet.

Included in the Humanitarian Center's 740 shipments in 2002 to four U.S. states and 19 countries were 152 Children's Institutional Modules and 88 pallets of toys from various sources.

"We always put 200 Happy Factory toys and a steam shovel in every Module we ship to orphanages, hospitals, clinics and such," says Humanitarian Center Manager William Reynolds. He adds: "Toys are not important from a volume standpoint. Nobody needs toys for survival. But they add to the quality of life for children. *The Happy Factory* is satisfying a hidden need - that of forgotten children. When a child gets a toy, there's a message - 'I'm remembered. I have value.'"

As the output of *Happy Factory* toys and special orders increased and more helpers signed on, Charles became concerned about potential liability. He telephoned Cedar lawyer and long-time friend Tom Higbee and started the conversation by saying "I'd like to talk to you sometime soon when you have a free minute."

"Don't ever talk to an attorney about a 'free minute,'" Higbee replied sternly and then laughed.

He first met Charles and Donna in 1981 when they lived in the same neighborhood and got to know them well over the years. He says "What I liked right off the bat about *The Happy Factory* was that it concerned kids plus Charles' and Donna's enthusiasm. They didn't retire to golf courses but worked full-time for nothing. They never took a dime."

Higbee felt their liability should be addressed and recommended incorporating *The Happy Factory* as a non-profit company.

"Can't afford it," said Charles.

"Don't worry about that. I'll do it," said Higbee, "and you'll need a 501c3 to satisfy IRS tax requirements. I'll get Jim Wilson [a certified public accountant] to handle that."

Higbee decided later that *The Happy Factory* name should be patented and had his friend Greg Madsen, a patent attorney in Salt Lake City, handle the details. It took two years to secure a ten-year patent and the renewal application had to be filed later. The $100 check for the renewal fee sent in by the Cooleys later was returned by Madsen.

He said "You guys don't have to pay."

Nor was any bill ever rendered by Madsen, Wilson or Higbee for services worth well over $2,000.

It wasn't the first time things happened that made Charles shake his head in wonder. He says "The Lord works in mysterious ways but I wish He'd tell me ahead of time what He's going to do."

Higbee served as Chairman of *The Happy Factory's* Board of Trustee until 2001 when he became a Judge of Utah's Fifth District Juvenile Court. He introduced the Cooleys to David Grant, President of Metalcraft Technologies Inc., explaining that "David reacted in typical fashion. When people hear about *The Happy Factory*, they automatically want to help."

Grant had moved from Salt Lake City to Cedar City in 1989 to purchase a sheet metal fabrication company that did work for Hallmark, which had a regional distribution center shipping out greeting card racks. When Hallmark changed its distribution strategy and decided to close their center down, Metalcraft switched to making parts for the aerospace industry.

Says Grant: "My first meeting with Charles was in Tom Higbee's office on February 18, 1999, and I remember two things about the visit - Charles' Hocus Pocus stick and Tom's request for a donation. I visited the original shed and was enthralled by what *The Happy Factory* was doing and by the Cooley's humble personalities. I checked with my partners and Metalcraft gave them five thousand dollars and an invitation to move in with us."

Charles elaborates about that generous help. "When I met Dave Grant, he asked what our plans for the future were. I told him that we someday needed to move to a larger facility in town because we had outgrown our shed where there was only room for me and two helpers and we were too far from town.

He said 'We just bought the Coleman building. Would you like to move in with us?' My chin dropped to the floor in disbelief. They donated the space, rewired it to accommodate our equipment, put in lights and the telephone and there was the new *Happy Factory*. We would not have grown without Metalcraft. Nothing was planned but Metalcraft was a catalyst."

Grant adds "It's not common to have a charitable operation sharing space in a commercial manufacturing plant but we had surplus space and were happy to help. It was good public relations for Metalcraft and got us pats on the back but we were motivated to help children, not get public relations value. *The Happy Factory* is something I believe in but we never dreamed it would grow and expand the way it has."

Moving day couldn't come soon enough for Charles and Donna. In mid-April, two months after getting the unexpected invitation from David Grant, they packed their scroll saw, table saw, band saws, sander, paint and hardwood scraps into their pickup and transferred operations to the Metalcraft building in an industrial section of Cedar City. There was not only ample space inside - almost triple that in the shop behind their house - but plentiful parking outside for more volunteers than they had been able to attract to their less handy semi-rural location.

Soon *The Happy Factory*, tucked into a 40' x 40' spare corner in the Metalcraft building, was producing more toys than ever before, and had become part of their landlord's standard plant tour.

Says Grant: "We never give a plant tour without a stop at *The Happy Factory*. Our customers are all happy to make that visit. Everyone gets excited and leaves talking about what they saw and the Hocus Pocus stick Charlie gave them."

"A Boeing Aircraft engineer couldn't figure out how it worked and I had to show him," Charles adds with a chuckle.

The Early Years

Charles and Donna Cooley in front of th first Happy Factory

"The Ship" Charles built.

Three of the 'Mother and Daughter' animal sets Charles sawed out and Donna painted.

Noah's Ark made for The 1998 Festival of Trees

(left) One of the Happy Factory flippers

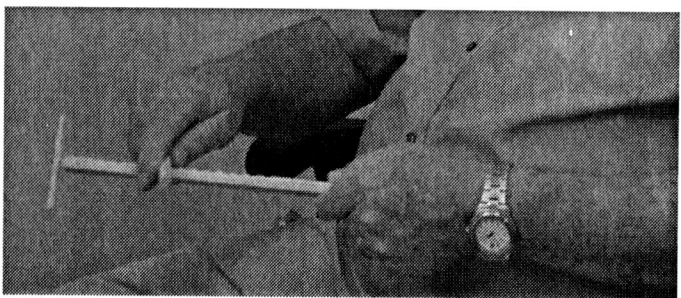

(above) Hocus Pocus sticks hoodwinked experts.

The Happy Factory - Ordinary people doing extraordinary things

Chapter 4 - The industrious elves of *The Happy Factory*

Magic was made daily behind the plain metal door in the simple, one story cement block building which sits in an industrial area of Cedar City, Utah.

It began on a typical Wednesday, June 25th, 2003, around 7 AM as the first workers arrived. They can be described with equal accuracy as a motley crew or an eclectic bunch, depending on your point of view, but they have a few things in common. Almost all are grey haired and wear some well-earned wrinkles, and every one of them is ready to contribute a few hours of time and talent to *The Happy Factory*.

The magic lies in what they make in the 40-foot-by-40-foot woodworking shop, tucked away in a corner, a dozen yards from the loading dock that serves a variety of other tenants who use this Metalcraft Technologies building primarily as a warehouse.

There's nothing passive or quiet about *The Happy Factory* which is soon alive with noise and motion as the volunteers begin to glue pieces of scrap hardwood together, trace patterns onto thick glued boards, cut out toy cars and trucks on band-saws, drill the holes that serve as 'windows' and hold axle pegs, sand them on all sides, box them ready for painting, and install wheels on those painted beforehand by other helpers elsewhere.

The Happy Factory where these volunteers show up week-days is as unlike any regular factory as you can imagine, and so are the workers. They come when they can and stay as long as they like. There are no bosses and no time clocks to punch. The hours for these self-starters and self-stoppers are completely flexible. Their production is un-metered and 'speed-ups' are unheard of. They work at their own pace, with neither great nor small expectations about their output, and there are no quotas, daily, weekly or monthly.

Their pay is in the best coin of all: total satisfaction with what they do and what is done in this special workplace. The finished products, painted and wheeled, are carefully inspected and then lovingly packed in cartons for delivery to underprivileged children all over the world. There's no charge. *Happy Factory* toys are always given away.

The first person to begin working the magic that Wednesday morning in June was Nathan Whittier, 20, the youngest member of the crew and Manager of the Wheeling Department. Nate is a regular and spends two to three hours every weekday morning at his specialty. He was a bit nervous at first about fastening wheels on the cars and trucks but soon decided it was the only job he wanted to do and it's a pleasure to watch him at work. He slides each wheel onto an axle peg, dabs the end of the peg with glue, inserts the wheel assembly into an axle hole in the wooden vehicle and, using a special jig, carefully taps it into place.

"I like this work," says Nate. "It's easier to do since I got muscle and it only takes me one minute to put four wheels on a car or truck. I've put 200,000 wheels on since I came to work here two years ago."

Every morning Nate looks forward as well to talking sports with Donna Cooley who arrives at *The Happy Factory* with her husband Charles a little before or a little after Nate does. (The Cooleys are long time friends of Nate's parents. His father, Bret, is the auctioneer who sold their twin goats, Itch and Scratch, for them for an astonishing price.)

The products dreamed up by Charles and Donna are what attract the volunteers, and the Cooleys are the glue that binds everyone and everything together. Just ask the first non-family worker to join the organization, Ray Baumgartner.

* * * * *

Baumgartner, 86, arrived in Cedar in 1943 as an Air Corps cadet and flew 25 missions as a B17 wing gunner in Europe during World War II. He was in Iceland, en route home to pick up a B29 bomber, when the atomic bomb was dropped on Hiroshima in 1945. He found his wife in Cedar and returned there after the war to work for Petrolane, a propane gas company, servicing refrigerators, and ended up in charge of five States and Alaska before retiring in 1984.

"I've been a woodworker since 1930 when I started in a high school shop. One thing I learned there was that one screw holds as much as ten nails," explains Baumgartner who has made all kinds of furniture over the years plus his special 'Chicken dinners' - two inch wooden cubes with a swivel top that opens to reveal three kernels of corn.

He continues his story. "I knew Charlie and his Dad, and started volunteering when *The Happy Factory* was still in the garage behind the Cooley's house. I loved the work and moved with them to Metalcraft. I do whatever needs doing - saw, drill or sand - on Mondays, Wednesdays and Fridays. I work ten to twelve hours a week for *The Happy Factory*, including time at home. I paint wheels there, 65 at a time with a spray can, and I've painted over 25,000 wheels."

Baumgartner took two *Happy Factory* cars to Anderson Lumber Co. in Cedar City to show the managers what he does, hoping to get a discounted price for spray paint. He did better than that.

"The lumber yard gets paint for half price - and gives it to me for nothing," he says.

* * * * *

Ken Boren, 67, retired after 33 years as a truck driver for Amerigas in Cedar City. His friend Jim Banks talked with him a long time about working at *The Happy Factory* but, until a year and a half before, he was having too good a time playing golf. Finally, however, he was persuaded to stop by.

Boren says "I couldn't believe what was going on. The good that was being done was just fantastic and I knew I had to be part of it."

"We come in Monday, Tuesday and Wednesday from 7 AM until 9 AM. I do a bit of drilling and sanding. I pick up boxes of scrap wood from Timberline Cabinet Doors on my way here

The Happy Factory

and take empty boxes back there en route home. The flexible hours are nice. You're free to do what you want when you want to," he explains. "After a year and a half, working at *The Happy Factory* is getting even better. We see the Thank You letters and videos and hear about where the toys went and how they were received. It warms your heart. I'll be here a while. I'm not going to retire from *The Happy Factory*."

[Ken Boren and Jim Banks customarily go home for breakfast and a shower after working at *The Happy Factory*, then go golfing together. But they are always willing to work 'over-time' if necessary. Banks was out of town visiting grandchildren and could not make it to *The Happy Factory* - or go golfing - this particular Wednesday morning.]

* * * * *

The sixth person through the metal door that morning, after Nate, Donna, Charles, Ray and Ken, was Richard Gunn, 81, former Chief Engineer, Morning Announcer and Assistant Manager of radio station KSUB in Cedar City..

Gunn retired sixteen years before, after 35 years at KSUB, and is one of the 'originals' who first volunteered when *The Happy Factory* was still in the Cooley's garage. Now he shows up Monday, Wednesday and Friday mornings around 9 and works for two hours. (Tuesday mornings he pitches horse shoes. Thursday mornings he gardens.)

He says "I try for six hours a week here, sawing and drilling. It's the kind of work that gets boring after two hours but doing something like this is therapeutic for me. It gives me something worthwhile to do. I sometimes ask myself 'Why am I doing this?' Then I remember that when I was a kid, I at least got one present for Christmas whereas the kids who get these toys have nothing."

Gunn is influenced by his experiences as a Staff Sergeant in the 9th Air Force in World War II. He contracted scarlet fever and spent 30 days in the isolation ward of a military hospital with no one to talk to. "That was the longest thirty days in my life. It seemed like a year," he says.

Later, during the Battle of the Bulge, he remembers Belgian children standing outside the air base fence holding empty buckets. "They had nothing to eat. We felt sorry for them."

Gunn and Ray Baumgartner both take *Happy Factory* rejects home, rework them to eliminate defects, and give them to neighborhood kids who, admittedly, are not deprived but have a liking for *Happy Factory* wooden cars and trucks.

* * * * *

Dr. Joseph Felix, 76, a teacher for 33 years at the Latter-day Saints Institute of Religion in Cedar City, and his wife Alene, 75, a self-declared "domestic engineer," have been on five missions abroad for the Mormon church since retirement - in Iceland, Cebu (the Philippines), Croatia (where they worked with Catholic charities during the civil war, helping to look after 600,000 refugees, and were evacuated twice) and New Zealand. These two-year missions were followed by two years teaching at Brigham Young University in Hawaii.

"It was tough work but somebody had to do it," says Joseph with an impish grin.

"There are many ways you can serve and those missions were a wonderful way to retire - until we found *The Happy Factory* two years ago. You get up in the morning, come here and feel better," he explains.

Joe and Alene spend two hours here, twice a week.

"I give the cars and trucks a thorough final inspection, making sure the wheels turn, the paint is up to standard and 'windows' have no burrs. Every child deserves the best," says Alene.

"I'm a cut up," adds Joseph, who prefers to operate a band saw at *The Happy Factory* and a fishing rod whenever he is near water.

Says Joe with a broad smile "I was tired and my wife retired. We have ten children, thirty-four grandchildren and five great-grandchildren. When we can't get to sleep at night, we count grandchildren instead of sheep."

* * * * *

West Goodman, 68, and his wife Meryle, 65, lived in California from 1937 to 1998. For most of those years, he worked in Hawthorne as an aeronautical engineer in Research & Development for Northrop Grumman, maker of the F-18.

With half their grandchildren in Utah and the other half in Arizona, they wanted to move closer when he retired in 1998 so they chose Cedar City as an ideal in-between location for their next home. Both like to garden and, says West "We're snow birds. We winter in Arizona."

The Goodmans heard about *The Happy Factory* from a neighbor and stopped by in 1999, shortly after the move from the Cooley's garage to the Metalcraft building. They work here two hours a day, five days a week. Meryle brands (with an electric branding iron) and installs wheels, and works an additional two hours each night 'wheeling' and painting the little wooden elephants that augment *The Happy Factory* product line-up.

"Meryle is one of our best painters," says a grateful Donna because good painters are hard to find.

"I do routing and make repairs, such as drilling out broken axle pegs," explains West. "Making toys for needy kids is a good thing to do. The Cooleys are dedicated to *The Happy Factory*. This is their life. But they can't do it all themselves. Supply is their big problem, not demand, and they are overwhelmed at times because they find it so hard to say 'No.'"

* * * * *

James Rasmussen, 72, retired five years before as a truck driver working out of Salt Lake City and Provo, Utah, and moved to Cedar City where a daughter lives. He heard about *The Happy Factory* from his wife who works with Donna Cooley in their church's Relief Society.

"My father was a carpenter and I've liked woodworking all my life. I started working here six months ago and try for four hours daily, three to four days a week. When I started, fourteen tubs of cars and trucks needed sanding. I sand because very few others want to do it. Every job is routine, even brain surgery, so you can be 'on vacation in Alaska' mentally while sanding toys," says Rasmussen.

"I remember how tough things were when I was a kid and getting my first toy, and that motivates me," he explains. "We have enough to live on. We don't need a job at Wal-Mart. My wife makes quilts [for the Relief Society] and I make toys. It makes you feel good to do something for others. I see pictures of foreign kids in rags scrounging for food on garbage dumps. It's unbelievable. We're so blessed to live in the United States. We have to give something back."

* * * * *

Tom Smith, 63, was formerly in the tree service business in the Los Angeles area, specializing in power line clearing and ornamental trimming. In December 2000, he and his wife moved to Cedar City because they liked its size and location as a mid-point between parents and children to the north, south and west.

After a family friend took their daughter to *The Happy Factory*, she urged him to volunteer.

"I didn't want to get involved but found I gradually had less and less to do at home and, five months ago, stopped by. Charles and Donna explained the flexible hours, I began cutting out toys, and absolutely loved it. You couldn't pay me to do this but I was impressed by the fact that no one makes a dime and the toys go to those who need them," says Smith.

His father lives with them, and his mother who has Alzheimer's is in a local hospital. His routine, five days a week: drive his father to the hospital, take a four mile walk, work for two or three hours at *The Happy Factory*, pick up his father and go home.

He explains "If I'm in town, I'm here. This is my ticket, the best way to give service. It makes my days more meaningful than puttering around the house."

On a recent trip to Los Angeles, Tom delivered 200 Happy Factory toys to the City of Hope, a giant hospital in Duarte, California, and got considerable satisfaction from transporting a cargo that was guaranteed to produce miles of smiles.

* * * * *

Mel Griguhn, 72, retired in October 1991 from the U.S. Army Depot in Tooele, Utah, as an electronics technician and technical writer. When his wife retired five years later, they headed south.

"Cedar doesn't get much snow and I moved here because I could play golf every day, year 'round," says Griguhn who concedes that he has become choosier about when he plays and might have become a 'fair weather golfer.' When his wife began picking up and painting *Happy Factory* toys at home, he began helping and, in spring 1999, went to work here.

"I've got to have something to do or I go crazy," explains Griguhn who puts in four to five hours a day five days a week in the winter and about half that in the summer, with golf fitted in between woodworking. He understudied Charles Cooley making the miniature steam shovels that were to become one of *The Happy Factory's* most popular toys [see Chapter 8] and quickly became the designated shovel-maker.

Mel says "In mid-1999, I cut out eight sets of parts and made eight shovels. Now we make ten at a time. When the order came in for 250 steam shovels in 2001, I thought 'Great, I'll build them, you deliver them.' I enjoy making them - it gives me a good feeling - and it keeps me busy."

* * * * *

Frank DelDuca, 42, is a Pennsylvania native with BSc degrees in Mechanical Engineering and Automotive Technology. He worked in Pennsylvania, Connecticut and Colorado before moving further west to the U.S. Army Depot in Tooele, then south to the red rock country of Cedar City where he discovered *The Happy Factory* and started work there in January 2001.

"I began by putting on wheels and sanding. Since then, I've done every process. Now I mostly build steam shovels with my buddy Mel Griguhn. *The Happy Factory* has helped to give my life meaning and purpose," says DelDuca.

He works here four hours a day, five days a week, and takes toys home to be painted. He is dedicated to *The Happy Factory* and what it does and says "I enjoy doing service and charity. Cedar is my home now and I'll probably work here for the rest of my life."

* * * * *

Earlier, when *The Happy Factory* was beginning to gather momentum, Charles Cooley had a long talk with an old friend, Leslie N. Jones, Professor of Psychology at Southern Utah University, and found the perspective he was given as exciting as it was enlightening.

"Most deprived kids live in a static environment. Everything is the same, day in, year out. A toy is a wonderful distraction from misery. It gives them hope and the impetus to use their imagination. Simple toys are much better than elaborate, structured toys which are models of the real thing and don't stimulate imaginations. They are what they are, whereas a box can be anything the child wants it to be," explained Dr. Jones. He added that "Self-esteem comes with what is done with a toy. A child figures out ways to use the toy that gives him or her a sense of accomplishment. The toy can do what they want it to do."

Dr. Jones continued. "Emotionally-traumatized children often suppress their pain and fear by turning off their minds. They stop thinking. The sights and sounds of their world only arouse despair. The most important elements of their life are beyond their control - they have no power - so they escape into a stupor of nothingness. But when they have a toy, they are in control. They have power. The simpler the toy, the more power and control the child has."

What Jones said made sense to Charles who likes to ask people rhetorically if they have ever watched a small child continue to drag a pull-toy, totally unconcerned, long after the toy has tipped onto its side and is not rolling on its wheels.

That conversation helped inspire *The Happy Factory's* Golden Rule: 'We take some wood that would be wasted, mix it with some time that would be wasted, and make a toy to stimulate a mind so that it won't be wasted.' Today, it's impossible to know for sure who gets the most pleasure out of *Happy Factory* toys, the people who make them or the children who get them.

The Happy Factory - Ordinary people doing extraordinary things

Chapter 5 - Invaluable scrap

What *The Happy Factory* does with scrap hardwood is so simple and so appealing that almost everyone who hears about the operation wants to help.

A case in point is Frank L. Cooley, 82, Charles' elder brother. Ironically, it was Charles, the amateur woodworker in the family, not his elder brother the master cabinet maker and builder, who co-founded and developed *The Happy Factory*. But however skeptical Frank might have been about Charles' woodworking ability and various projects, he was always supportive, and his hard-earned expertise always came in handy, whether sawing angled ends on roof rafters for a mountain cabin or critiquing the paint job on a train for Kristine's kindergarten class.

During World War II, Frank became a Sperry Bomb Sight expert before enlisting in the U.S. Army Air Corps. Postwar, he and a buddy formed a construction company to build houses in Cedar but folded it after three years of thin profits. He worked for a lumber company and finally settled for a career with a Cedar City cabinet maker.

Although theoretically retired, Frank is as busy as ever in the large shop behind his home in Cedar which holds an impressive collection of machinery.. He maintains *The Happy Factory* saws, sanders and drill presses and, if anything goes wrong, it rarely takes Frank long to get things back in working order. And he joins and glues hardwood (usually oak) boards together before sawing them into cab parts for *Happy Factory* steam shovels or, using an ingenious home-made rig, band saws them into beautiful circular steam shovel bases which get a final finish on a surface planer and sander in Paul Cozzens' shop.

Cozzens, 41, mentioned briefly in Chapter 3, is another example of the response to *The Happy Factory*.

Cedar City's housing market was dead in August 1987 when he founded his company and began making high-end custom cabinets and furniture.

"To survive, we had to get a license to operate in Nevada, and our first major job, as a sub-contractor, was the Lamb residence in Las Vegas," Cozzens explains. "Since then, we've relied on word of mouth advertising and an ad in the Yellow Pages. Eventually we were able to buy our present building and double our space to 10,000 square feet."

Cozzens had worked with Frank Cooley and heard about Charles who he met accidentally one day in 1998 in the hallway of the Latter-day Saints church they both attend in Cedar. He liked what he heard about *The Happy Factory* and began supplying scrap board ends and ordering wooden wheels for the little cars and trucks from Saunders Brothers in Maine.

The savings were substantial - 26 cents for four wheels and four axle pegs compared with the $1.22 Charles had been paying - but the minimum quantity was 10,000 and *The Happy Factory* had no credit. Result - Cozzens Cabinets LLC absorbed the cost of wheels and pegs which, in less than two years, more than doubled to $7,600.

Cozzens didn't complain. He says "I honestly never missed the money. My wife and I had a vision. We thought what *The Happy Factory* was doing was worthwhile. We have been blessed and you can never get square with the Lord."

Yet demand for *Happy Factory* toy parts continued to grow and the sums had become so large that a new deal was called for by the Cooley's tax accountant who insisted that commingled accounting was not appropriate, accurate or fair for either Cozzens Cabinets or *The Happy Factory*.

Charles readily agreed, explaining that "We'd already ordered close to one million wheels and axles and were ordering more every month."

In January 2003, with Paul's help, *The Happy Factory* opened its own account with Saunders Brothers and began paying its bills directly, while Paul and his wife arranged to make other contributions to their favorite non-profit toy makers.

But Cozzens' help was more than financial. In 1999, as previously noted, when *The Happy Factory* demand for wood exceeded the supply available at his shop, he introduced Charles to Mark Messer at Timberline Cabinet Doors in Cedar.

"Mark was reluctant at first because he didn't think small board ends would be useful. But he didn't turn me down and, after several months, he realized the great contribution he was making and caught the vision," Paul said.

Messer admits that putting aside wood was a bit of a bother at first. But a routine was worked out and, before long, three to five boxes of hardwood board ends were going to *The Happy Factory* every week. Today he laughs at himself.

"I'm a tightwad. I don't like to throw anything away. The first pickup load of 2 ½ inch strips I gave Charlie had been accumulating for years. We were tired of tripping over this scrap and decided it was time for a house-cleaning," Messer said, adding that *"The Happy Factory* has made it easier for me to get rid of stuff and keep our shop cleaner and I don't have to haul away scrap. It's a win-win situation for both of us."

Another of Paul Cozzens' good deeds cannot be forgotten. He and the Cooleys had become friends and allies and, one Friday afternoon in August 1999, four months after *The Happy Factory's* move into the Metalcraft Technologies building, Charles stopped by Cozzens Cabinets wearing a long face. One of *The Happy Factory* band saws had died and the other was dying.

Paul immediately went into action. "I don't really deal with Delta [Machinery] but I telephoned their 800 Customer Service number and was referred to Liz Pollock at Delta headquarters in Memphis, Tennessee. I told her about *The Happy Factory* and its need for new band saws. She said 'We don't do that sort of thing' and wasn't very encouraging but asked me for more information so I FAXed her seven pages about what *The Happy Factory* was doing for the needy kids in the world. I called her back three days later, as requested, and was astonished to have her tell me they had already shipped two band saws!"

Ms. Pollock had consulted with her supervisor. Impressed by the seven page plea for help, he had authorized the shipment of two 14-inch Delta band saws worth around $1,500 retail.

"It was incredible," says Cozzens. "I asked her how often they did things like this and she said 'We've never done anything like that before!'"

A few *Happy Factory* toy cars and trucks Donna sent Liz Pollock as a Thank You ended on her desk. When Marikay Jung from Delta's Pittsburgh office visited headquarters, she was so taken by them that she and Liz reportedly spent much of the morning 'carpet-testing' little cars and trucks on the office floor. Later, Ms Jung wrote, asking how to secure toys for needy children in a Pittsburgh hospital she supported. Donna sent her a box of cars and trucks as a gift, explaining they were not for sale, and was pleasantly surprised to receive a generous donation for *The Happy Factory* from Ms. Jung.

As *Happy Factory* production continued to expand, Cozzens Cabinets and Timberline Cabinet Doors combined could not supply enough wood, and Paul thought of a possible new source - Lumber Products (LP), one of his main wood suppliers and an employee-owned, civic-minded company with headquarters in Oregon. In late autumn of 2000, he put thought into action when Larry Mortenson, LP's Assistant Manager in the Salt Lake City office, stopped by on a sales call, and gave his visitor a pitch for *The Happy Factory*.

The story was compelling and convincing. "At the time," explains Mortenson, "we had some below-grade, sappy cherry and, on Paul's say so, we delivered a lift of that wood to *The Happy Factory* in December."

There was almost 2,000 square feet in the lift, worth over $7,200, and Cozzens is still shaking his head in wonder, explaining "We could have used at least 70 percent of that cherry. The quality was that good."

The timing was equally spectacular. A few months later, *The Happy Factory* found itself buried by the Utah State Office of Education's huge order for steam shovels. Says Charles: "We were struggling to find wood, and the Lumber Products lift really put us in the steam shovel business. We used it for steam shovels only."

On their next trip to Salt Lake City, the Cooleys stopped by Lumber Products to express their thanks and deliver a toy steam shovel to show how the wood was being used. When Mortenson saw the steam shovel, he called in his colleagues to have a look.

"They couldn't believe what we had done with their cherry wood and said they would see what they could do to help," Charles says.

The steam shovel was left on display in the Lumber Products office lobby "as a sample" and, a few months later, when LP Industrial Sales Manager Ross Atkinson and LP Industrial salesman Walt Lowry were in Cedar, Paul Cozzens took them to visit *The Happy Factory* and meet Charles and Donna. They were impressed by what they saw and heard.

"We spend so much time making money and worrying about ourselves that, to see people concentrating on helping others, was really touching," says Lowry.

"I was awed that anyone would do for others what they were doing. Charlie's stories moved you to tears. Since then, *The Happy Factory* has always been in the back of our minds," Atkinson adds.

That first truck load of cherry marked the beginning of a wonderful relationship between a worthy cause and a generous company. "Whenever we have off-grade material, we think of *The Happy Factory*. It's a neat organization. We think it's a great thing to bring a little happiness to troubled children," explains Mortenson, who gets regular updates about *Happy Factory* activities.

So roughly twice a year, when Lumber Products cleans up its Salt Lake City yard, a load of wood is trucked to *The Happy Factory*. "Some of the boards are twelve and fourteen feet long," report a grateful Charles Cooley. "Lumber Products is the main source of our steam shovel wood."

More help, of a different kind, was equally unexpected. For several years, *Happy Factory* steam shovels had been getting a free ride in Deseret Industries' trucks from Cedar to the

Humanitarian Center in Salt Lake City. However, they were loaded loose and subject to scuffing or worse damage en route. None of those sent to the Utah State Office of Education (see Chapter 8) were in boxes and Charles decided there had to be a better way for them to go.

In early 2002, he visited the Western Container Division of Longview Fiber Co. in Cedar City and talked with an engineer there about securing shipping cartons that would fit the steam shovel. He left a sample with him and, a few days later, the engineer called back.

"Would you like to see what we've done?" he asked.

Longview had designed a sturdy, double-walled shipping carton that fit a steam shovel perfectly. Plant Manager Cliff Maxfield explained to Charles that a minimum production run was 500 units and the price would be $2.18 per carton for a total of $1,090, a hefty sum for *The Happy Factory*. But after checking with his Board of Trustees and getting approval for the expenditure, Charles ordered 500 and, a week later, a Longview truck arrived with 500 form-fitting cartons.

A delighted Donna Cooley took delivery and asked politely for the invoice.

The Longview driver shrugged. "Don't have one."

Puzzled, she telephoned the company and was told "There will be no charge."

"I choked up and about cried and said it's really hard to say the proper Thank You for your goodness to us," Donna said.

The next day, a grateful Charles went to Longview and delivered thanks in person.

"We need to do things like that," said Maxfield.

Other organizations had different needs. For example, painting toys proved to be good therapy and good karma at the Southwest Utah Youth Center (SWUYC), a multi-use correctional facility with short-termers who stay 6 to 7 days in one wing and long-termers in a second wing. The second wing is a 10-bed unit for 12 to 20 year olds - all males, convicted of a variety of crimes, from assault and burglary to armed robbery and murder, who are incarcerated for one year or more.

. The program there began in 1998 after Charles spoke at a

Lion's Club meeting in Cedar about *The Happy Factory* which was still operating in cramped quarters in the shed behind the mobile home. A member of the SWUYC Advisory Board was present and impressed, and invited him to address the Board which subsequently decided to experiment by letting long-termers help make *Happy Factory* toys to earn restitution money.

Juvenile Courts in Utah order the parents of youths in custody to pay for some of their care. Part of these involuntary contributions go into a restitution fund which is tapped to pay the wayward youths the minimum wage for work done in the correctional facility. The Courts then disburse these earnings to their victims as restitution.

The work available for inmates is limited, and SWUYC head Jay Maughan felt they might prefer to paint toys rather than mop floors and scrub walls.

"A lot of the kids in here are right-brained. *Happy Factory* work stimulates their creativity and adds meaning to their restitution," says Maughan, adding that "We started with sanding and painting, under supervision, and we supplied the materials. We have a higher counselor-inmate ratio than adult prisons, three to one at times, and eventually we acquired two band saws and a drill press which three or four inmates were permitted to use under supervision." Initially, Scot Goulding, a counselor at the Center with a background in carpentry, was put in charge, and began making regular visits to *The Happy Factory* to pick up unpainted toys and deliver painted ones. He explained that the inmates had to earn the right to paint and really like it.

Says Goulding "We always have good painters and it boosts their self-esteem to do a good job". Seven hours of restitution per week are required but there's no regular schedule. Some kids have free time to paint on Saturdays or Sundays. Others paint an hour a day after school. Sometimes someone will make a big mess with a paint job and has to be warned that he risks losing his right to paint but there have been no major problems."

He adds that "I used to get *Happy Factory* newsletters and

The Happy Factory 48

letters received from organizations which got *Happy Factory* toys and read them to the kids. Some told me that, while they were painting, they thought about the children who would get the toys. Once we had a couple of kids who painted a marijuana leaf and other inappropriate things on toys and the other kids protested, saying that underprivileged children didn't need that sort of thing."

"*Happy Factory* work gives back. The toys have a worthy purpose," Maughan says, citing the positive feedback from his charges who, when asked, say such things as 'I like doing something for needy kids' and 'It makes me feel worthwhile.'

The toy painting program was expanded to include putting wheels on the cars and trucks and, when the power tools were added, to cutting out toys as well. "It was a big time privilege for an inmate to use the saws. They had to gain our trust," Goulding says.

Output at the Southwest Utah Youth Center varies but averages around 40 finished cars and trucks per month.

Since help for *The Happy Factory* repeatedly came from different directions, the Cooleys were not surprised to get a telephone call in 1999 from Allen Julian when he was supervisor of inmate placement at the Utah State Correctional Facility in Cedar City. Julian had learned about *The Happy Factory* from his wife, who worked with Kris Cooley in the Enoch Elementary School, and sensed an opportunity for prison inmates to provide a bit of useful public service. Because of security concerns, he says "the only thing inmates could do was paint." Even this posed problems since paint could be stolen and used for artistic but illegal in-prison tattooing, while stolen brushes could be sharpened into weapons.

Nonetheless, Julian got approval for the basic plan and the next step was securing supplies and supervisors. About fifty-nine dollars in profits generated from pay phones and commissaries in the prison were used to buy paint and brushes and Wayne Mifflin, principal of the local Iron County Adult High School, agreed to have two of his teachers show inmates how to paint and supervise them.

The Happy Factory

The Cooleys welcomed Julian's offer of help and gave him 100 unpainted cars and trucks to take to the Correctional Facility. The initial reaction there surprised him.

"Half of the 82 inmates said they didn't have the time. Can you believe that, inmates without spare time! But the other half volunteered to paint and, when the first 14 signed up, the class was full because that's all the small room set aside for painting could hold," explains Julian.

They painted for one hour each weekday and often would come back after school was out to paint some more. The opportunity to paint was also made available to female inmates who plied their brushes in the evening.

Julian is still surprised by what happened. "The meanest man in the prison, a cantankerous old timer, 71 years old and a murderer who had spent most of his life in prison, complained bitterly when told to paint toys. I threatened to keep him in prison forever if he didn't cooperate. A week later, he told me he'd never felt so good in his life and said 'Sign me up for the rest of my life.'"

"It took two months to paint the first 100 toys, then Daniel Black, a high school instructor, began painting with them. Before long, hardened criminals - murderers, rapists and child molesters - were begging to paint toys, and that old con led the charge. I think they all saw it as a way to pay back society, although they didn't grasp the concept at first and the quality was very poor. Then they saw photographs supplied by Charles of African kids getting *Happy Factory* toys, and had a change of heart. Some cons are great tattoo artists and they said to themselves 'Ah, we'll use wood this time instead of skin.' I saw it as therapeutic and exchanged the painted toys for another hundred unpainted ones. Things soon reached the point where I was delivering and picking up one hundred toys every month."

Julian adds that precautions were necessary. "Tattoos are a status symbol for some inmates. They help establish a pecking order in jails. And since regular tattoo ink is not available, inmates will use anything they can get, and they love colorful metallic paint. Cons are ingenious in substituting and improvising. For ink they would burn paper, catch the soot and scrape it onto a table for the tattoo artist to mix with water. They would take the motor out of a Walkman and use it to drive a tattoo needle. Since needles are shared, the infection levels are unbelievable. And, if caught, they're locked down for 90 days."

Budget cuts forced the Correctional Facility in Iron County to close on September 16th, 2002, and the last toys were returned to *The Happy Factory* two months before that. The toy painting experiment was not continued for a number of reasons. Senior state prison administrators were unaware of the Iron County program. Someone with clout was needed to spearhead such a project, and attempts to convince bosses up the chain failed.. Volunteer instructors needed to supervise the painters were scarce. The paint and brushes raised security problems. And enthusiasm varied. Early in the program, after a box of 100 toy cars and trucks was taken to the Garfield County jail, it took six months to get them back.

"It didn't work there," says Julian.

What did work was a one-man program featuring Ken Benson, a lifelong friend of the Cooley's and Donna's former boss at Southern Utah University. In 1975, he got Parkinson's disease which became steadily more debilitating and finally left him in a nursing home, unable to speak clearly and badly crippled, with little muscle control.

Charles says "We'd visit Ken a couple of times a year and felt so sorry for him that one time, in 2000, I took him a box of 10 wooden cars, 40 wheels and axle pegs, a mallet and glue and showed him how to insert a half axle peg in each wheel, dip the end in glue, and hammer the wheel and axle peg onto a car. He struggled and struggled and couldn't do it. I left the box with him anyway and, a week later, got a call from the nursing home. 'Ken needs more cars.'"

"The next visit I took him 25 cars and a hundred wheels and axle pegs. Two weeks later I got another call. 'Ken needs more cars.' Before long, I was taking him 25 cars every week Then it got up to 50 cars a week and 100 cars a week. Ken was a big, stubborn man and he made himself put those wheels on those cars. He couldn't talk but he had an old Royal typewriter and somehow managed to hit enough of the right keys to make himself understood. One day he typed out "Thank you so much. I've finally found something I can do. I'm going to spend the rest of my life putting wheels on wooden cars for little children who don't have toys."

In a letter to the Cooleys in 2001, Ken's daughter, Shelley Goodwin, wrote "Rarely in life something or someone comes along that makes every day more wonderful. You are those kind of people and *The Happy Factory* is that special 'something.' We searched and prayed and tried zillions of things that hc could do that would be useful and yesterday, when I went to visit him, he was engrossed in putting wheels on *Happy Factory* cars. He was consumed by the project. My heart was full and I think his was, too."

Donna adds that "Ken didn't like the mallet we brought him so Charles' brother Frank made him a special mallet with a rubber grip and a sturdy work table with a wooden top on a pipe frame. He must have put wheels on eight thousand to ten thousand cars before he died."

"Ken wheeled the last toy on the day he died in August 2002," says Charles. "When his son stopped by the nursing home the night before he died, there was a car on the work table with two wheels on it. The next morning, when they found him, all four wheels were in place. It was probably the last thing that proud and stubborn old man did."

How tender loving care makes Happy Factory toys

Match up wood scraps, add a giant dab of glue, and clamp tight

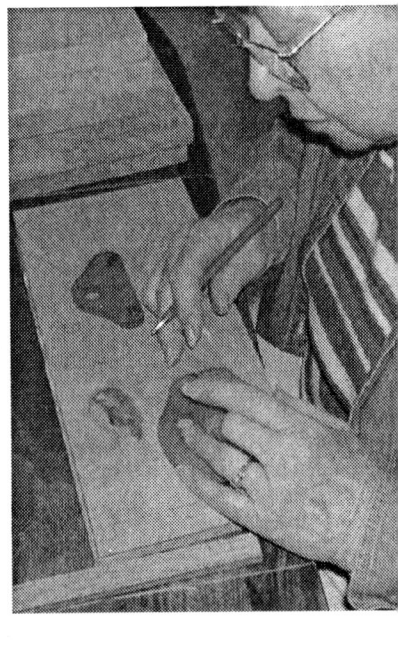

trace patterns

and saw precisely

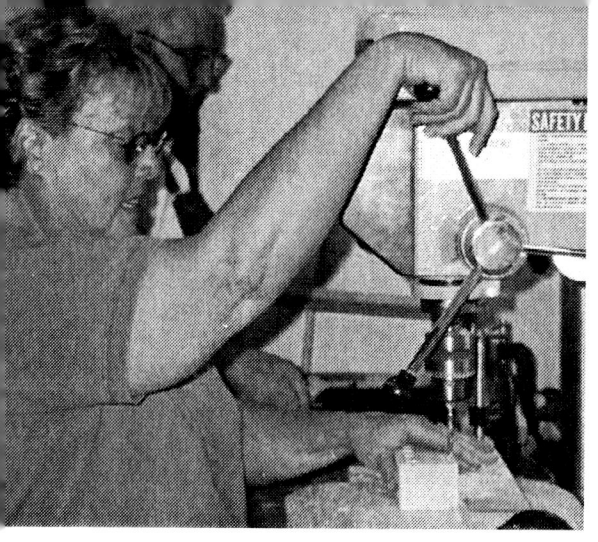

Drill axle holes and windows

and off all the rough spots

Rout off sharp edges

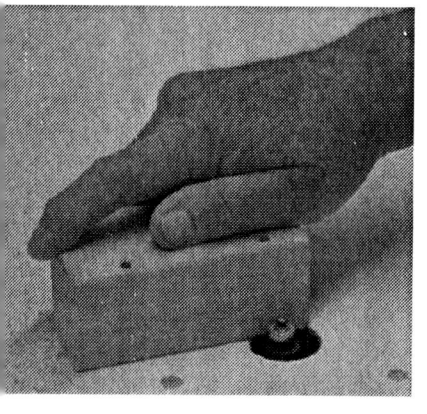

for the stamp of approval

 Oil finish for some,

paint for others

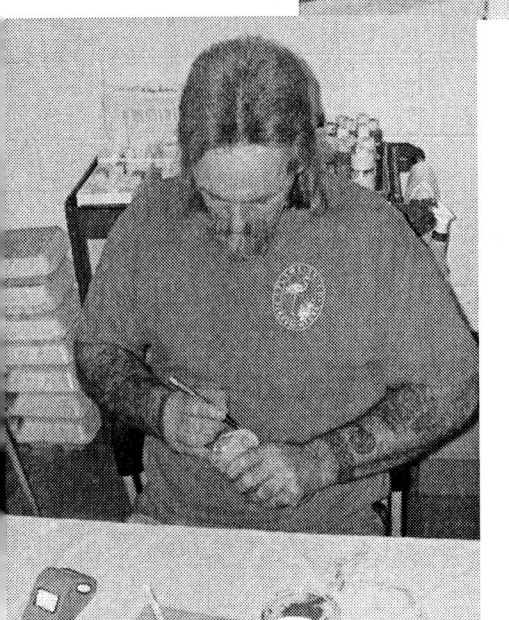 with delicate final touches

Teamwork gets the job done

The Happy Factory - Ordinary people doing extraordinary things

Chapter 6 - A benevolent virus

Dramatic expansion, as unplanned as almost everything else that had happened, got underway only a year and a half after the Las Vegas craft show launched the Cooleys into their second career as toy makers to deprived kids of the world and only a few months after inspiration produced *The Happy Factory* name.

The idea of taking wood that would be wasted and mixing it with time that would be wasted to make a toy that would stimulate a mind so it would not be wasted was contagious. No one had put the pieces together so effectively until Charles and Donna Cooley came along. What they began accidentally in Cedar City soon started to spread like a benevolent virus in all directions, nationwide at first and eventually internationally.

In the spring of 1997, during a visit to the Humanitarian Center, Bob Bement, 50, a salesman for Chemcentral, and his wife Ann, were attracted to a wooden toy branded *The Happy Factory* and asked where it was made. Three weeks later, on a business trip to Cedar City, Bement telephoned Charles from his motel and was invited to the Cooley home where he found wooden toys everywhere. After a talk with Charles and a tour of the workshop out back, Bement decided he wanted to be a part of it.

"How can I help?" he asked.

The Cooleys were startled. They had not given a thought to anything more complicated than producing toys in the shop behind their house but, as their visitor explained later: "We clicked."

Bement had a fully-equipped woodworking shop in the basement of his house in Woods Cross, a few miles north of Salt Lake City, and they spent the evening discussing the basics of starting a *Happy Factory* branch. The fundamentals were simple enough. The second *Happy Factory*, like the first, had to be a non-profit, charitable operation. The toys would be given to children in need and none would be sold. The Bements would secure their own wood and make what they could when they could, with no production quotas to meet. The Cooleys agreed to supply patterns, band saw blades, wheels and axle pegs.

Back home, Bement found a local cabinet shop willing to donate scrap wood and an enthusiastic wife, eager to participate. Before long, *Happy Factory* #2 was in operation.

"We didn't plan to have a branch of *The Happy Factory*. It just evolved," says Ann Bement. "I had never worked in the shop but, when I saw the cars, I thought 'Hey, I can do this,' and I was excited. It was fun when you knew you were making 'little miracles.'"

She and Bob sent a letter explaining their toy-making plans to neighbors, and three couples pitched in with help. However, the neighborly interest flagged and, after a year and a half, she says "There were just the two of us left producing cars."

In the early days, the Bements made time to produce around 1,000 cars and trucks each year and, in addition, supplemented the Cooley's help for the Shriners Hospital in Salt Lake City. Right from the start, the Bements were ready and able to fulfill special requests covering a wide range of unique needs, from an adjustable table desk and an easel-mounted peg board with knob-shaped pegs to a box with a mirror on top (because so many children responded to a mirror) and a scooter board with directional casters. When physical therapists called, the Bements responded promptly with such things as a pair of elevated handles which permitted a young boy to exercise on his own, and a wedged ramp which helped a five year old boy with cerebral palsy strengthen his head and neck.

Later they got some outside help with toy production. Every six weeks or so, two men, each working in his own shop, began to bring in a bag of cars, ready to be painted. But the biggest problem was finding quality painters. Hundreds of little cars were ruined by sloppy painting. Sanding them down and re-painting them was more trouble than starting from scratch so they usually ended up as firewood.

"It's been a learning experience," explains Ann. "I think many people underestimate how much work is involved and are embarrassed when their paint jobs turn out badly."

The Bements now limit production to one model, the sedan, painted a solid color, and spruced up with wheels painted by a young lady who comes by regularly and does 200 at a time. Distribution has been the easiest part of their operation. Some toys go to a local hospital and a local homeless shelter. Most are delivered to the Humanitarian Center.

With seven children, three still living at home, busy lives became even busier for both Bements and output has gradually slowed to around 500 cars per year.

"My work is hectic and my side job is demanding," says Bob. "Our *Happy Factory* does not have the burning priority it once had but we're still making toys and, time permitting, will continue to make more."

* * * * *

In mid-1999, Roland Anderson retired after 40 years as a general contractor, building houses and commercial buildings in northern Utah. He'd read about what *The Happy Factory* was doing and contacted the Cooleys about establishing a *Happy Factory*.

"I had a lot of time on my hands and a well-equipped shop," says Anderson.

A bit later, the Cooleys stopped by for a talk, pegged him as an ideal choice and, in July, he began making toys.

The retired contractor, then 79, was born and raised in Richmond, Utah, 13 miles north of Logan near the Idaho border. He learned the builders' trade from his father, a farmer and electrician, and his grandfather, and remembers being paid 20 cents an hour as a senior in high school to teach wood working to fellow students.

During his years as a contractor, Anderson made cabinets in the large cement block shop behind his house in Richmond, equipped with an impressive range of power tools from table saw, band saw, radial-arm saw and chop saw to jointer, thickness planer, shaper, router and several sanding machines.

"My hobby was making Grandfather Clocks and caskets," explains Anderson, who has a sample of each, superbly crafted, stored in a side room off the shop. Over the years, he figures he's made 25 caskets and 50 clocks in his spare time, all meticulously finished, with a fancy design trim etched on each clock front using a small router bit and a piece of his wife's lace as a pattern.

Now he applies his skills, experience and tools full-time to toy-making. He's in the shop from 8 AM until 6 PM weekdays and from 8 AM until noon on Saturdays. Until mid-2002, when a neighbor began volunteering two to three hours a day, twice a week, Anderson worked alone. Another volunteer signed on more recently and puts in three hours a day, three times a week. And from the beginning of his toy-making operation, his sister has stopped by regularly to hammer wheels on all the little vehicles. His wife Alice despairs of ever getting the shop clean let alone keeping it that way but, every work day, she sweeps clear a sizeable patch of floor by the side door leading to the house.

"We put out about four hundred wooden cars and trucks each week," says Anderson who takes pride in his original designs for a pickup truck, Model T car, sedan, school bus and other vehicles. "I can always use more help but I don't want to be obligated."

Anderson has had no trouble finding people willing to paint, and has acquired a unique stable of talented painters. Inmates of the Cache County jail and the Franklin County jail, mostly non-violent law-breakers with an indiscreet drug habit and ample idle time, execute intricate designs with tender, loving care.

"The Sheriffs stop by once a month to deliver 100 finished toys and pick up another batch, and the neighbors may wonder why I get so many house calls from the law," says Anderson with a grin. He adds that the polyurethane clear coat finish is sprayed on by a jailer out of doors, well beyond sniffing range of the inmates.

Sorority and fraternity members at Utah State University in Logan show up regularly at the Richmond shop as well, to deliver painted vehicles and pick up unpainted ones. And a Senior Citizen Center has become a source of "competitive painters" who strive to out-do each other in the fit and finish of their painting.

But getting wood has been a problem. Says Anderson: "For years, I made a 90 mile round trip to Tremonton every six weeks to get material and had just enough to keep going until, not long ago, my supplier went out of business and I ran out of wood. I prayed for material and the next day a man called from a molding mill in Logan and asked if I could use some wood. A semi-truck load of hardwood strips arrived shortly after, along with a promise of more any time we needed them." He adds "We've been discovered. They'll keep me in material."

Distribution is the easiest part of Anderson's operation. Toys from *Happy Factory* #3 are given regularly to local hospitals and a trauma center. Numerous charities make Christmas requests and receive a box of 150. Almost every other Thursday throughout the year, a Deseret Industry truck picks up 900 to 1,600 toy cars and trucks and hauls them 95 miles south to the Humanitarian Center in Salt Lake City. In addition, Mormon missionaries have been making direct deliveries to orphanages in several countries including Argentina, Mexico, Rumania, Russia and South Korea as well as the United States.

"All they have to do is let me know where there's a need," explains Anderson. "One couple took two boxes of toy cars to the Appalachian region of Tennessee. There were people there as bad off as any elsewhere in the world."

He says his annual operating costs are "at least $500, maybe a thousand if I figure in travel." In addition to utility bills for the shop, the main expenses are for sanding discs and belts. Longview Fiber in Logan donated 200 cardboard boxes, and is expected to provide more when needed.

* * * * *

The Happy Factory 57

1999 was a vintage year for Happy Factors.

It was then, much to their surprise in 1999, that the Cooleys received a flurry of calls from other would-be toy makers who had heard good things about *The Happy Factory*. Exactly how and where was not always clear but the Associated Press wire service pick-up of Ed Kociela's report was undoubtedly partly responsible (see Chapter 7). After simple contracts were signed, factories #4, #5 and #6 were opened by J.D. Webb in Round Rock, Texas; Gene Ham in Mesa, Arizona; and Richard and Arlene Outcalt in Corvallis, Oregon. In November, George Throop started making toys in Sierra Madre, California, on the edge of Pasadena, raising the total to seven.

Throop, 76 at the time and a native of Pasadena, had for 53 years run the building materials company founded there by his father. World War II interrupted his studies at the University of Southern California and, after a three year stint in the U.S. Army, he joined the family business. He helped it diversify from a supplier of lath and plaster into landscaping materials, lumber and high tech concrete, mixed on board specialized trucks and delivered to job sites in precise quantities. Major customers included contractors patching California freeways.

On a visit to Cedar City during a deer hunting trip in 1990, George and wife Nancy were introduced to Charles and Donna by Nancy's brother Lanny who lived across the street from the Cooleys and volunteered now and then in *Happy Factory* #1. Additional visits to Cedar strengthened the Throop-Cooley friendship and George became more and more impressed by what Lanny's neighbors were doing.

He explains that "I didn't have any wood-working experience but something touched my heart and I wanted to make toys for needy children so I took a night class in carpentry."

Finally, Throop phoned Charles about opening a *Happy Factory*. Shortly thereafter, patterns arrived. A scroll saw, drill press, sander and router were purchased, and George was in business, a non-profit one this time. His first delivery, a box of 40 toys in late 1999, was a cold call on the City of Hope Cancer Center and Hospital complex, which he calls "the bald head capital of the world."

Other visits to the Center were less joyful as he passed control of the family business over to two sons and began his fight against non-Hodgkin's lymphoma, a three year battle that ended in 2003 with the cancer in remission. That April, at the annual City of Hope reunion of cancer victims, George was the oldest patient to have received stem cell treatment.

"Even when he was sick, George went into his garage shop as a diversion. Toy-making was good therapy," explains Nancy.

"Now that I'm feeling better, I spend about twenty hours a week in the shop," George says, adding that a life-long friend comes by every Wednesday afternoon for a few hours to help out.

Thirteen different wooden toys are produced in Happy Factory #7, including ambulances, buses, jeeps, trucks, dogs, rabbits, ducks and elephants, and a major problem has been neatly side-stepped. "We don't paint. Every hospital nurse I've talked to prefers bare wood toys the kids can paint and take home," says George.

Nurse Gayle Cox at City of Hope adds "The kids really like painting - or splattering - the wooden cars and trucks. This is a strange place, with six or ten people poking and probing them, and the toys help take their minds of their fears. The toys are something positive that says 'this is not all a bad place.'"

Lynda Farnworth, a Child Life Assistant at Huntington Hospital, explains that "Bed-ridden children are offered a *Happy Factory* car to paint and take home. They can be quite creative and sometimes paint two or three as extras, to be left behind. They love them and the toy is theirs."

Throop uses lumber remnants from the family business as stock to produce 120 toys each month, and delivers a box of 40 every two months to six different hospitals in the Pasadena area, including City of Hope and Huntington. It seems fair to say that toy-making has given him a new lease on life.

"I'm just going to do what I'm doing. It's the best therapy in the world. I'm happy as a clam, at peace with the world," says George with a broad smile.

* * * * *

In February 2000, with the ink barely dry on Throop's contract, engineering consultant and former Professor Paul Tullis opened *Happy Factory* #8 in Logan, Utah.

"We were in St. George and my wife, who is a real bird dog, had read an article in the Christmas 1999 issue of Family Circle magazine about *The Happy Factory*. She bugged me to call Charlie and I did. We talked and shortly afterwards I started making toys," Tullis says.

Toys are a far cry from his profession. He was born and raised in Ogden and, after getting a BSc and Phd in civil engineering in 1961 and 1966, taught at Colorado State and Utah State for 33 years. This included a hectic period from 1977 to 1980 when he was on the faculty of both universities at the same time. His specialty is hydraulic engineering, involving pipes, valves and pumps, posing such problems as vibration and cavitation, and he spends about 30% of his time traveling worldwide as a consultant for a number of clients.

One trip took him to Saudi Arabia where water is more expensive than oil and a desalinization plant was malfunctioning. Another time he was called in when engineers at Cape Kennedy were having trouble with the valves that failed to open and flood the pad with tons of water when missiles are launched.

But Tullis has a shop under his garage and an assortment of tools.

"Most are left over from the time when I worked for three years with my father who was a contractor building schools and small commercial buildings," he explains.

These include a Delta Unisaw, thickness planer, 6" jointer, 14" band saw, two drill presses, edge sander, router and a dust collector to offset allergies.

What he did not have was a supply of wood, and sometimes the pickings have been lean. In the summer of 2002, he picked up four loads of scrap wood from Dixie Woodworking in Salt Lake City but the company subsequently went bankrupt and he's on the lookout for another source.

Tullis and his wife Sherry are deeply involved in other

charitable works including sewing projects and he says his main problem now is finding time for toy-making. They spend about 400 hours a year sewing quilts and blankets, and collecting and buying clothes and shoes for donation to the Humanitarian Center in Salt Lake City.

"Each month I'm in the shop about twenty hours and what gets me back there is a call from a church with a service project. But we don't paint anymore. We deliver bare wood cars and trucks covered by three or four clear coats of water-based polyurethane, with sanding in between coats. The toys are more durable and more consistent and it saves time," he explains, adding that "I usually put the wheels on."

At one time or another, four people have helped Tullis with the toy making. "They last about three visits. Nobody catches the spirit. But I still invite people to participate who I feel might benefit," he says.

The annual output from *Happy Factory* #8 is around 2,500 cars and trucks, and most are delivered to the Humanitarian Center for shipment anywhere in the world there is need. But he and his wife report that one of their most memorable experiences was supporting a five member family who took humanitarian aid, including 200 toy cars and trucks, on a mission to South Africa.

"If people only knew the lasting joy that comes from leaving the world a little better than they found it," says Sherry Tullis.

* * * * *

Bruce Bone, born in 1933, is a Utah native and U.S. Air Force veteran who worked as an inspector for the federal government and a Procurement Specialist for an association of five Utah counties. A year after retiring in 1993, he moved to Manti, in southern Utah, with his wife Penny, a self-described "service brat" raised on numerous military bases.

She says "When Bruce retired, he wanted to make wooden toys for our grandchildren and we turned our carport into a garage and shop. I was very sick then and he was going crazy. He'd work 15 or 20 minutes on the conversion, then run into the house to check on me."

One way and another, the conversion was finished in three months. A neighbor donated a drill press, the Bones bought other tools and more have been added as birthday and Christmas gifts. Eventually, the grandchildren had all the hand-made toys they could handle and their son-in-law, who had worked for Charles Cooley at Southern Utah University, told them about *The Happy Factory*.

Says Bruce: "I needed stress relief and golf was not it. I liked working with wood and in February 2000, Penny and I went to see Charley. The idea appealed to us so we worked for a couple of days in Cedar learning how to make wooden toys, then signed an agreement to follow the *Happy Factory* rules, which include not selling anything and taking care of local needs first."

Family members (the Bones have 9 children and 13 grandchildren) and friends help out now and then, but toy production in their Manti workshop is basically a twosome. Every month Bruce works about 30 hours and Penny 15 or 20 hours, making 12 different toys and 8 puzzles. He mainly glues boards, saws, drills and sands. She traces patterns, puts on wheels and, concedes Bruce, "Penny does a better job than me cutting out the toys and puzzles."

Their output in the three years ending January 15, 2003 was 2,200 toys.

For Bruce, who has had four heart attacks and open heart surgery, toy-making has been therapeutic. He says "I can go out in the shop and, in a few minutes, I'm relaxed." However, he adds somewhat sheepishly that "Charlie imposes no quotas but I put quotas on myself."

"He creates his own stress. I have to tell him 'That's enough!'" declares Penny.

Almost all the wood the Bones need is donated by 'Custom Cabinets by Brent' in Manti. Their main problem has been painting which is farmed out to volunteers.

"We emphasize quality over quantity and most people do a great job. It's fun to see what their imagination has created. However some groups took our toys and had kids paint them. We don't want to hurt people's feelings but we've really had to tighten down. People are told what they are painting may be the only toy a child will ever have, and are given precise instructions [on do's and don'ts]," Penny explains.

Their toys go to a variety of organizations. Hospitals give a red helicopter to children on 'life flights.' Ambulance crews have found a *Happy Factory* toy calms a frightened child. And Emergency Medical Technicians give children a toy ambulance if they or their parents are hurt.

"A neighbor's child got a pink car before having her tonsils removed and that was the first thing she asked for after the operation. When she took it home, her brother tried to take it from her but failed," says Penny.

Bruce adds: "*The Happy Factory* has been a blessing for us, not only to keep my stress level down but to be of service. As I work in the shop, I can just picture a smile on a child's face."

* * * * *

The *Happy Factory* branches continued to multiply even though the Cooleys never advertise or solicit. Happy Factors are all volunteers, a unique cast of strangers unknown to each other and, in most cases, unknown initially to the Cooleys as well. But all are determined to help.

Participation is no picnic and, when some of the callers learn what was expected of them, they do not call back. Toy-making is time-consuming and repetitive, a bother and sometimes a burden. The work is all give and no take. No one is paid. There is no profit to be made. The Cooleys provide patterns, bandsaw blades, axle pegs and wheels, and the electric branding iron that burns '*The Happy Factory*' onto each toy. Otherwise, Happy Factors are on their own, driven by a strong commitment to make toys and give them away to needy children. That was, is and will always be enough.

"Happy Factors are free to make the toys they want to. We find the less we meddle, the better things go, since we're dealing with volunteers," says Charles Cooley.

It was not possible to talk to all of the Happy Factors, but those who signed on after the Bones were as diverse as the earlier arrivals. All kinds of people, from a chemicals

The Happy Factory

salesman, contractor and engineer to an English teacher and a retired barber, have opened branches. They have little in common other than a delight in making needy children smile. The following examples are typically atypical.

*   *   *   *   *

In December 2001, Edward and Morrissa Rich were in their Salt Lake City home watching a short television news report about *The Happy Factory* and said to each other "We could do that."

Ed, then 59, is from New York state and a computer programmer who runs his own company. Morrissa, originally from Wyoming, teaches English part-time at a local business college. They emailed Charles and Donna Cooley and met them the next weekend in Salt Lake City.

"They are wonderful, gracious people and were interested in expanding their toy-making operations. I was struck by how few demands they made. No quotas, no time frames. I can only work on weekends and holidays, and the low-key approach made it possible for us to establish a *Happy Factory*," says Morrissa. "In January, we decided to go ahead."

The Richs had a 24' x 36' shop, still under construction in their back yard, equipped with basic wood-working machines. It was built originally to make furniture and provide household storage and lacked a heating and air conditioning unit. This limited production to the pleasant temperatures of spring and autumn when Morrissa estimates she puts in four to ten hours per week.

She says "I work at toy-making in spurts. My first real effort was two weeks during the 2002 Winter Olympics when the college was shut down. I worked hard and made several hundred toys and trucks."

Estimated production the first year of operation: 800. The shop will have heating and air-conditioning when Ed finishes a re-wiring job but no significant increase in production is foreseen since the same time constraints will remain.

Their toys have ended up in interesting places. Intrigued by a TV newscast one evening about a local motorcycle club that took toys to needy children, Morrissa telephoned and was asked to deliver hers to the Barbary Coast Saloon in downtown Salt Lake City. No sign identified the biker bar and the door was marked by a small slot reminiscent of a Prohibition-era speak-easy.

"We were admitted but hardly anyone took notice of us at first. When they did, we felt the motorcyclists were more surprised to see us than we were to see them. But they were wonderful, and grateful to get the box of 50 *Happy Factory* cars which were given to Shriners hospital," says Morrissa.

Another time, when a Thanksgiving weekend trip shrank unexpectedly to one day, the Riches drove 60 miles east to Roosevelt, Utah, consulted the local Yellow Pages, then delivered 18 toy cars to the local Crisis Center and another 18 to the hospital which serves the local Ouray Indian Reservation.

Their biggest order so far came from the Utah Tole Painters Guild, a group of talented women who asked for 150 cars and painted them "exquisitely. They were little works of art, like Faberge eggs," says Morrissa, and were delivered to the Humanitarian Center.

Production, from gluing scrap board ends together to band sawing, drilling, sanding and routing, is handled solo by Morrissa. She says "We're concerned about liability and have chosen not to have people come to our shop so I do everything but paint." And sloppy painting, by eager but untalented volunteers, has been the main problem.

"Half of the 125 toys recently returned had to be sanded down," she explains. "I will have to limit painting to three or four people I trust."

Other problems? "The shed has now probably cost $35,000, not the five or ten thousand we originally counted on, but that's our fault," says Ed with a laugh. "For the *Happy Factory*, we only had to buy a 6 inch sander and a router. Cash needs are insignificant. Our main contribution is time."

Scrap hardwood is contributed by a local cabinet shop. When employees there, mostly Mexican immigrants, learned

The Happy Factory

that many *Happy Factory* toys are given to needy children in Mexico, they told their boss good-naturedly "Give her ALL the wood."

Why bother running a *Happy Factory*?

"We saw a definite need and had the ability to meet it. They are good little toys, with integrity, and I like making a quality product. Even a rich kid would like a *Happy Factory* car," says Morrissa.

* * * * *

Founding a *Happy Factory* is not always straight-forward and easy. Witness the misadventures of Alton and Cheryl Thacker.

These high school sweethearts, both born in 1935, were raised on hard-scrabble farms in the Duchesne County foothills of the Uinta Mountains 60 miles east of Salt Lake City and, to the dismay of their parents, married at 17. Despite the overwhelming odds against the success of teenage marriages, they made theirs last.

Al worked in construction as a heavy equipment operator and, says Cheryl, "One year we moved thirteen times. Our longest stay in one place was six weeks. But we were young and had never been out of Duchesne County and we were seeing the world."

Al somehow managed to fit barber school into the schedule and in 1961, when the first of their eight children turned five and started school, he began barbering for $1 per haircut at Brigham Young University (which had offered Cheryl the four year scholarship she had given up to marry him). He continued to work in construction summers and says "I made as much money in those three months as I did during the nine months at BYU."

He opened his own barbershop in 1970, expanded his hair piece business, took a hair styling class (paid for with a $425 inheritance from his father) and won several stylist competitions before retiring from barbering 27 years later.

In 1981, the Thackers became seriously involved in charitable giving after an optometrist told them about the desperate need in Mexico for eyeglasses. Since then, they have collected and delivered over 40,000 pairs of glasses on annual trips south of the border. On a visit to Mexico in 1995, they met Tim, a 7 year old boy with cerebral palsy, fed through a tube in his stomach. He was the inspiration for the Tiny Tim Foundation they established the following year as a charitable channel to help him and other unfortunate children.

In 1999, the same year they bought a comfortable three bedroom condo in Salt Lake City, they ran across *Happy Factory* toys in Nueva Casas Grande, Mexico. On their return to Utah, they introduced themselves to the Cooleys and were given 1,000 toy cars for Mexican children. After stopping several times on trips north and south to work a few days in the Cedar City Happy Factory, the Thackers decided they needed one of their own.

Al explains that "The Cooley's toy production was limited and we couldn't get enough cars for our Mexican projects."

Signing on was easy. "If you don't like it, you can quit. If we don't like it, we'll lift your branding iron," said Charles.

The hard part was finding the right place to make toys, and getting started. In an 18 month search around the Salt Lake City area, Al found six possible properties, including a former polygamy compound at the mouth of Little Cottonwood Canyon. But the owners would not or could not grasp what *The Happy Factory* was all about. Skeptical landlords all wanted $1,000 to $1,500 a month plus a security deposit and several hundred dollars more for utilities.

"We couldn't afford that kind of rent," says Al.

The Thackers were about ready to give up their dream when, in 2002, his sister Lorna spotted a house for sale in Sandy, a Salt Lake City suburb, with a backyard big enough for a *Happy Factory*. The structure, once used as a halfway house, had been empty for two years and was in sorry shape.

After an inspection visit, Cheryl told Al "I'd only consider that house if we could swap it for our condo." To her astonishment, the owner soon called and asked if they would trade their condo for his house. "I concluded that this was what we were supposed to do and this was where we were supposed to be and here we are," she explains.

Before completing the swap, Al took care to get approval of their project from their neighbors as well as the blessing of Sandy City officials and, in June 2002, the exchange was made. A 26' x 28' aluminum frame structure with steel cladding soon rose from a thick new concrete pad, with the building and much of the equipment donated and all of the work done by volunteers.

The official opening September 14th was covered by Salt Lake City's TV Channel 13 with two telecasts which triggered over 50 telephone calls from people interested in helping.

Unfortunately, few actually appeared, and fewer still showed up more than once and became regulars, even though the workplace is cheerful, the tasks are undemanding and the hours could not be any easier: 'Come when you can, leave when you want to.' Consequently, *The Happy Factory* #19 labor force has been limited mainly to Al and Cheryl, family members and three or four men and women who come in to work several hours each week.

Other setbacks were discouraging as well. Although there has been no shortage of volunteer painters, the quality of painting has ranged from beautiful to abominable. Then, three months after the factory opened, evening work had to be discontinued as a result of unreasonable complaints from a new neighbor who moved in next door.

Yet the Thackers remained undaunted and kept their sights set high on one of the most ambitious production goals imaginable. For Al, *The Happy Factory* became virtually a full-time job. From Monday to Friday, he was in the shop most days from 7AM until 5:30PM and, despite the obstacles, toy production steadily rose and often reached a remarkable 1,000 finished cars and trucks per week.

Distribution posed no problems. On the receiving end have been local hospitals, Jordan Valley School for severely disabled children, Indian children living on grasslands at the bottom of the Grand Canyon and the impoverished children of Ascension, Mexico. And no day went by that he and Cheryl didn't think about their payoff - the broad smiles on the faces of children when they receive a *Happy Factory* toy.

(The spiteful neighbor won. On April 19th, 2004, Sandy City officials caved in to the spurious complaints, reneged on their original promises and closed down the Thacker's *Happy Factory*. Fortunately, the climate in West Jordan, another Salt Lake City suburb, was more salubrious and *Happy Factory #19* is back in operation there.)

* * * * *

There are now 26 Happy Factories - 24 in the United States, one in Brazil and one in the United Kingdom - with more undoubtedly coming.

Charles Cooley says "I can see how *The Happy Factory* evolved. The toys were a by-product. *The Happy Factory* is a way for people to do something meaningful. Thousands of people have contributed tens of thousands of hours making hundreds of thousands of toys. There's no way we could have planned what happened."

He continues: "It's strange. I've never even met many of the folks who run *Happy Factory* branches except on the telephone. Yet when I get a call from someone interested in establishing a *Happy Factory*, I can tell instantly whether it's likely to work. I feel I've known the person for years. If you put all the Happy Factors in a bag, you could pull any one of them out and find they were basically all the same. I can't tell them apart."

Some of the supporting cast

undreds who keep

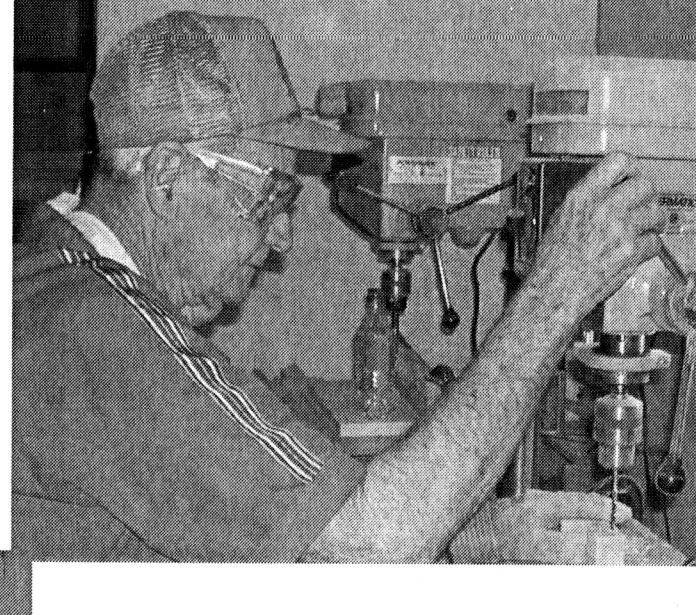

the Happy Factory humming.

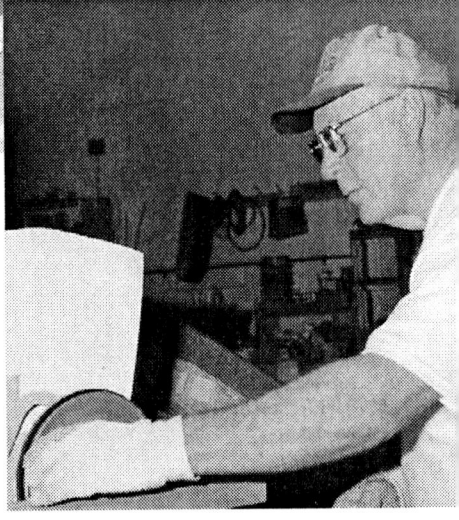

A sample of Happy Factors

at work-

or play

The Happy Factory - Ordinary people doing extraordinary things

Chapter 7 - A chain reacts

The chain reaction of support and goodwill generated by *The Happy Factory* continued to add new links in unexpected ways and the cast of characters expanded.
 The word was getting around that a couple in Cedar City were doing wonderful things with scrap hardwood, and people were curious to know more about what was going on. The Cooleys were invited to address the luncheon meetings of service clubs such as Rotary, Lion's and Kiwanis, and they spoke to several Senior Citizen groups, attracting more volunteers at each talk. One elderly man was so enthusiastic that he ended up walking 2 ½ miles every Wednesday afternoon just to paint toys.
 A little extra giving also advanced the cause and concept. Two *Happy Factory* steam shovels donated to Primary Children's Medical Center's annual Festival of Trees in Salt Lake City in 1997 immediately attracted handsome bids. The next year, the Cooleys cut out 39 pairs of animals, each pair made from different exotic wood from all over the world, to occupy a Noah's Ark Christmas tree at the Festival. In addition, they donated a Nativity scene made from the same exotic wood, a rocking Hardly Davidson, Irish mail car, red wagon and steam shovel which together raised over $7,000 for the Medical Center (including $2,500 for the Hardly after two determined gentlemen got into a bidding contest.)
 By the end of 1997, the Cooley duet had grown into an ensemble of helpers from 8 to 80 years of age best described as eclectic. The volunteers included daughters, friends, neighbors, families, school classes, Boy Scouts, Girl Scouts, youths from three correctional facilities, senior citizens "and anyone else who wanted to participate. We stood amazed at

how many doors had opened and didn't know of any other way we could have had such a positive effect on so many children," says Donna.

By that time, the Cooleys were not only delivering toys to Primary Children's Medical Center and Shriners Hospital in Salt Lake City. They had connected as well to the Southern Utah University branch of Head Start, a nation-wide organization which provides educational, health, mental health and nutritional services to children with special needs in low income families.

The SUU branch is responsible for seven counties in southern Utah where there are 22 Head Start centers, each with paid staff looking after 17 to 20 male and female four year olds. These under-privileged children attend special pre-schools 16 hours a week, taking classes in English as a second language, math, science and art to help them compete with their peers later, when they enter the public school system. Their parents meet at the centers once a month and are encouraged to help with the planning.

"Even the worst parents try to help their children," says Enrollment Specialist Darlene Storie.

Happy Factory toys were an extra bonus for Head Start students and often became special treasures. A four year old boy in Cedar who fell in love with the elephants he saw in a parade when a traveling circus came to town was given a little wooden *Happy Factory* elephant, which he carried everywhere in his backpack. Later, after his family moved to New York, he was badly injured in a traffic accident which left him hospitalized and in a coma for several days. The first thing he asked for when he finally awakened was his elephant. Family and medical staff agreed that the wooden elephant probably helped his recovery as much as medicine.

In December 2000, the SUU Head Start leaders decided to fill a Christmas stocking with food and other necessities, including a toy for every child in the 22 southern Utah centers. But they ran short of funds.

Darlene says "I was desperate. The children were not going to get toys. I called *The Happy Factory* and Donna gave us

400 cars and trucks."

This was the beginning of a new Christmas custom in Cedar City. Early in December each year, *Happy Factory* toys are delivered to Darlene's Head Start office. There, with a list in hand, she picks out toys for the children in each Center and puts them in bags which are unloaded into stockings at the Centers.

"The children get almost as excited as we do when they see *The Happy Factory* toys," she explains, adding that the gift, valued at $7,500, not only delights several hundred children but adds an extra measure of Christmas cheer for the staff by qualifying the SUU Head Start branch for $7,500 in matching federal funds.

* * * * *

Without missing a beat in their toy making schedule, the Cooleys made time for important visits, some out of town. Early in 1998, they drove 40 miles south to the Snow Canyon Middle School in St. George, Utah, at the request of Randy Yardley who was teaching three Grade 8 shop classes. Several boys in each class did not have enough money to buy material for their wood-working projects and Yardley asked the Cooleys if they could help. He was pointed toward several St. George cabinet shops willing to donate scrap wood, and given patterns, wheels and axle pegs in case any of the boys were interested in making *Happy Factory* cars and trucks.

"They delivered several dozen toys and Mr. Yardley was really thrilled. He explained that making a simple toy teaches more different shop techniques than building a shelf would require," Charles said.

* * * * *

The non-profit Canyon Creek Women's Crisis Center in Cedar City, one of 16 in Utah, was another early member of *The Happy Factory* fan club.

Victims of domestic abuse who show up on their own at the crisis center, or are delivered by a police officer or legal advocate, can count on a safe shelter for 30 days or more.

About half arrive with children and little else. Typically, there are 150 to 170 women and children in residence plus 200 more 'out patients' who get counseling.

"We have a great big house with eight bedrooms with bathrooms, and a communal kitchen, living room and playground. We try to make it cozy and warm and there's no charge for any services," explains Executive Director Anne Yero. "Women often reconcile with their abuser but the longer a woman is battered, the more likely she will fight back, and I've given some women 90 days of shelter."

Director Yero was pleasantly surprised when the Charles and Donna knocked on her door in May 1998, told her what they were doing and asked if there was any need for toys.

"Yes!" she answered enthusiastically.

Shortly after, the Cooleys returned with 25 cars and trucks, following up on a third visit with 25 more plus a steam shovel. These toys are parked in a living room closet and a child who becomes attached to one of them can take it home. The 'missing' are periodically replaced and, at the Christmas party every year, the stockings hung by the chimney with care each hold a new *Happy Factory* car or truck.

"We receive a variety of toys, including stuffed animals, but *The Happy Factory* cars and trucks are special. They are unique and more personal. They don't look commercial. They're not Wal-Mart. And toys are such a comfort for children, providing emotional therapy as they become engrossed with them," says Yero.

* * * * *

In mid-July of 1998, Janeal Jones introduced herself to the Cooleys with a telephone call and then drove from St. George to Cedar to pick up and paint 50 toy vehicles and 50 flippers.

[Footnote: *The Happy Factory* philosophy is simple. 'If you have a need, you qualify for a toy.' Asked what happens if someone lies about their need, Charles says "That's their problem."]

Three weeks later, Ms. Jones returned the toys, beautifully painted, and picked up some more. When they got to talking,

The Happy Factory

she mentioned corresponding with an aunt and uncle who were LDS missionaries in the Ukraine. When she told the Roger Henricksens what she was doing, they emailed back, asking if some of those *Happy Factory* toys could possible be sent to needy children in Kiev.

The Hendrickens wrote "At the hospital we visited last week, the children had no tables, chairs, TV or toys, only bare rooms with beds. There's a big playroom with nothing in it but a bare floor."

On their next visit to the Humanitarian Center, the Cooleys passed Ms. Jones request on to Lloyd Pendleton who called in Kevin Nield, a Field Operation Manager. Serendipity was once again at work. Nield was taking a shipment to Kiev in September, knew the Henricksens, and promised to include toys for them to distribute.

* * * * *

On November 2nd, 1998, Janeal Jones telephoned again, asking whether she could have 300 toys for an orphanage in Hermosillo, Mexico. She needed them by November 23.

Charles said "Of course you can have them."

The Cooleys were up to their elbows in Christmas orders, and figured some extra long evenings would be needed to fit in this unexpected order. Fortunately, two weeks before, daughter Jolene had spent two days cutting out 400 of the exact kind of toys needed for the orphanage. It still took 3 ½ days of sanding, routing and oiling to finish the order but Ms. Jones got the toys to Hermosillo well before Santa Claus arrived.

* * * * *

With the first delivery of some *Happy Factory* toys, Christmas in 1998 was merrier for children in the Ronald McDonald House in Salt Lake City than it might have been.

Ronald McDonald Houses provide a home-away-from-home for families with critically-ill children receiving care in nearby hospitals, and there are over 200 in operation world-wide. The first House opened in Philadelphia in 1974, largely as a result of efforts by Fred Hill, a Philadelphia Eagles football player whose daughter had leukemia. Hill realized families with hospitalized sick kids needed an inexpensive place to stay, and enlisted the help of teammates, the Eagles' owner and Ray Kroc, founder of the McDonald's restaurant chain.

Kroc donated $50,000 toward the first House. Since then, the Ronald McDonald House Charities has provided each new House with 'seed money.' But all are independent, operated and funded locally.

In 1988, the 100th House was built and opened in Salt Lake City, offering 29 bedrooms, each with private bath. Most are for two people. Some can sleep three. Two units are specially designed for disabled guests. Families are referred to the House by personnel in the hospital where their child is being treated. There are no means tests. Guests pay a nominal $10 a night and can stay for a maximum 30 days, although the rules are flexible and neither condition is rigid.

The Salt Lake City House has a communal kitchen with four burner stoves, refrigerators, dishwashers, sinks and counters. Pantries hold a variety of donated food and, for in-house meals, guests need not buy groceries, although many do. Adjacent to the kitchen is a spacious dining area. Elsewhere in the house are a living room, TV room and recreation area. A second Salt Lake City House, opened nearby in 2002 for families needing to stay more than 30 days, has 15 one and two bedroom apartments.

Those using the Houses must live at least 50 miles away from Salt Lake City and have a sick child 18 years old or younger. Since opening, the Salt Lake City Ronald McDonald Houses have served more than 15,000 families, some from as far away as Argentina and Bosnia. Many have healthy children who appreciate *The Happy Factory* toys and are permitted to keep their favorite, some found in Sub-for-Santa bags at Christmas.

In 1999, a wooden steam shovel and two boxes of toys were a hit at the Salt Lake Houses' Mardi Gras silent auction held to raise money for the Share-a-Night program to help guests pay for their accommodation. More *Happy Factory* toys have arrived since then in what's become an annual tradition.

*   *   *   *   *

A letter from Shandra Powell, Director of the Family Support Center of Southwestern Utah in Cedar, adds another perspective:

"On Tuesday, March 9th, 1999, I was scheduled to work the over-night shift at the Family Support Center. We had six children in shelter care and I was the only staff member available to spend the night with them. I did not sleep during the night as I found myself rocking and comforting a three year old girl and a six year old boy who were missing their mother terribly. Needless to say, it was a long night.

"I was relieved at 7:30 Wednesday morning. As I checked my desk calendar before leaving, I saw that I had a 9AM appointment to tour *The Happy Factory* Workshop. My first impulse was to call and reschedule but I remembered that this was a rescheduled appointment and I felt the need to follow through. To be honest, I was not looking forward to the visit.

"I arrived at 9AM and was immediately greeted by two of the most energetic, caring people I have ever met. Taking the short tour and hearing about the love that went into the making of the *Happy Factory* and the toys you distribute was almost overwhelming. While I was there I also overheard a very loving mother comfort her adult daughter who had been ill. I sure did need that jolt of compassion. It is very easy for me to get sidetracked by the sadness I see on an almost daily basis but I was reminded that there truly are decent, loving people who go overboard to honor children.

"Thank you so much for realizing that it is not our responsibility to make our children worthy of the world, yet to make the world worthy of our children."

* * * * *

Several weeks later, soon after operations moved into the donated space in the Metalcraft building on April 23rd, Ed Kociela stopped by *The Happy Factory* and unexpectedly spread the good word nationwide.

Kociela, Senior Writer and Columnist for the <u>Cedar City Daily News</u>, moved. to Cedar in 1983 from El Segundo, California, where he worked for the <u>Los Angeles Herald</u> and the <u>Los Angeles Times</u>. He and his family had vacationed in the Cedar area two years before and liked what they saw.

"We were tired of being penned in by the violence and restrictive environment in California but friends thought we were crazy to move to Cedar City and live among 'those people,'" says Kociela - who was not and is not a member of the Church of Jesus Christ of Latter-Day Saints. "We were turned on by the security, culture, warmth, friendliness, diversity and emphasis on family values here. And this community inspires anyone interested in the arts. You're encouraged to make creative efforts. Some of this rubbed off on the Cooleys with their idea of trying to supply every needy child in the world with a toy. They would have been laughed at in LA,"

Kociela was curious. He had heard about *The Happy Factory* and the deliveries to shelters, crisis center and hospitals. His first reaction was "Do these guys know what they've got, since I've seen pricey shops in southern California where their steam shovel would sell for at least five hundred dollars?"

"I asked myself how can the Cooleys afford to give their toys away? People in southern Utah don't have deep pockets. You hear lots of stories about charitable operations but most can't be sustained, and fail. I visited them in their little shop, without the tools, wood or volunteers they had later, and thought 'What wonderful people and yet they're going to fall flat on their tails,'" Kociela says.

But he wished them well and wrote a story about *The Happy Factory* for the <u>Daily News</u> in Cedar City which is a bureau of the <u>Spectrum</u> in St. George. To his surprise, his June 27th, 1999, story was picked up by the Associated Press (AP) and put on their national news wire which reaches subscribing newspapers all over the United States. The next thing the Cooleys knew, they were flooded with telephone calls from almost every state in the union, praising them for their good works, seeking more information about *The Happy Factory* and sometimes asking how they could help.

"When Ed's article was picked up by the Associated Press, it seemed like the whole world opened up to *The Happy Factory*," says Charles.

"The miracle was in the conception - and incredible, unlikely things happening," Kociela says.

The unknown pair of Cedar City toy makers had abruptly become known, not by any means like Donny and Marie Osmond and other members of Utah's famous musical family, but the subject of a gracious introduction by AP to all kinds of people, both the curious and the caring.

The publicity, totally unexpected, was turned to good account by Donna who talked with the callers and explained *The Happy Factory's* need for painters.

She says "I found out who they were, what organization, if any, they represented, and gave them a big spiel about our emphasis on quality."

She checked as best she could on the bona fides of each telephone caller before sending him or her a box of 100 cars, and reports that 99.9% of them came back - and still come back - well-painted, adding that "Our standards are high and we're tough about rejecting sub-standard painting. We tell them 'If you're not sure whether it's good enough, then it isn't.'"

The new volunteers supplied their own paint and brushes, and paid all shipping charges from and to Cedar. Today *The Happy Factory* has a stable of trustworthy 'repeat painters' and, at any one time, there are approximately 7,000 toys out being painted at various locations around the United States.

* * * * *

Later in the summer of 1999, the Cooleys were startled to learn they had won an award they did not know existed, for which they had no idea they were competing.

Connecticut-based Swiss Army Brands, in partnership with National Geographic Adventure Magazine and the Outward Bound Wilderness program, had spent the first half of the year traveling around the United States looking for people who were "Swiss Army Equipped." This they defined as inspirational and aspirational people who serve as role models and heroes - "ordinary people doing extraordinary things."

While their choice for the first ever Swiss Army Equipped Award - Charles and Donna Cooley - was undisputed, the date of the presentation could have been a little less memorable in other ways. The honors on August 12, 1999, were interrupted by a noon-hour tornado which the National Weather Service rated F2 (meaning winds were up to 157 miles-an-hour) that tore a swath through downtown Salt Lake City where merchants specializing in outdoor gear were displaying their goods, destroying the Swiss Army Brands tent and many others.

Unfazed by Mother Nature's fury, the sponsors moved everything a few blocks north to the Utah State Capitol grounds, unscathed by the unusual winds. Company President J. Merrick Taggert explained that the award was given to recognize inspired people who exhibit resourcefulness, ingenuity and a spirit of adventure in overcoming challenges.

The Cooleys were lauded for raising the spirits of children in need with donations of nearly 12,000 Happy Factory toys, and were presented with a sterling silver Victorinox Original Swiss Army knife and a $2,000 scholarship in the Outward Bound Wilderness program in their name for a deserving teenager of their choice. They sought help from Cedar City friends in finding a candidate and, after a difficult struggle, finally narrowed their choice to two worthy local boys. Then they stalled, unable to decide. Taggert solved their dilemma by generously funding two scholarships instead of one.

The boys, Evan Fox, 15, and Helaman Haynie, 14, both Cedar City natives who had never seen a stretch of water larger than Lake Powell, flew to Maine in August 2000 and spent two weeks on an adventure with a group of 20 young girls and boys, learning to row, sail and navigate two 28 foot open deck sail boats in the Atlantic Ocean. The trip, designed as a challenge and exercise in survival, involved such novelties as spending 24 hours alone on a small island with a bag of gorp (like trail mix only less edible) and a water bottle, and rappelling down a cliff as well as taking turns as captain for a day on board a sail boat.

Helaman confessed to his parents later that the food was so unappetizing he was tempted to ditch it until his stomach reminded him of his father's favorite proverb: 'Hunger is the best sauce.' Both Helaman and Evan were thrilled by their experience on land and sea and, when they returned home says Charles Cooley "They weren't little boys anymore."

* * * * *

Kociela's story on the AP wire opened all kinds of windows on the world outside of Cedar.

The Cooleys had barely recovered from the Swiss Army Brands award (and the tornado) when Margaret Jaworski, a Family Circle editor, telephoned from New York on August 25th. She had read about them and wanted to do a story about their *Happy Factory* in the magazine's December 1999 issue.

Understandably surprised by the show of interest from a national magazine, the Cooleys responded to her request for more information by shipping off a few *Happy Factory* toys and several newspaper clippings about their activities. Receipt of the supporting evidence confirmed Jaworski's news judgment and she responded with a second call, reaffirming her interest and the need for photographs. Black Star photographer Tim Kelly phoned a week later to make an appointment and arrived in Cedar soon after that to spend the better part of a day pointing his cameras at the Cooleys wearing what Donna calls "the funny elf hats."

Ms. Kaworski couldn't make it to Cedar for a face-to-face interview with the Cooleys but called several more times to tidy up details. Family Circle published a two-thirds page report in the Christmas issue which reached the news stands on November 20th, spreading the word about *The Happy Factory's* good deeds further, triggering more telephone calls, and helping to attract more Happy Factors (see Chapter 6)

The herd instinct among magazine editors is noticeable where good feature stories are concerned and word of Family Circle interest in the Cooleys passed around New York publishing circles. On November 17th, Cathy Free called, wanting to do a *Happy Factory* story for People Magazine's Christmas issue, due out in four weeks. She was shipped sample toys and newspaper clips and interviewed the Cooleys by telephone. A few days later, Steve Smith, a free lance photographer from Sun Valley, Idaho, flew to Cedar, showed up at *The Happy Factory* with two red and white Santa Claus hats and devoted the afternoon to another photo shoot. To Charles' and Donna's amusement, he made sure they handed back the Santa hats.

Early in December, the Cooleys got another call from New York. A disappointed Cathy Free was on the line.

"They've pulled my story!" she said, explaining that a disastrous fire had pre-empted her less timely *Happy Factory* report and assuring them it would run a year later - and it did.

* * * * *

Press and television reports continued to generate interest but the plaudits and kudos never interfered with the basic *Happy Factory* mission of toy-making. The focus was still on Primary Children's Medical Center, Shriners Hospital and the Humanitarian Center but the list of other deserving recipients was expanding. No attention was paid to geography, race, religion, color or creed. The only criteria was need.

Toys for the playroom and playground were delivered to the Volunteers of America detoxification center in Murray, Utah. More toys went to the Esparaza De Los Ninas Orphanage in Mexico, St. Jude's Cancer Hospital in Memphis, Tennessee, the Women's Crisis Center in Tuba City, Arizona, and Honduras and Belize, both battered by Hurricane Mitch, and others.

The typical give-and-take was beautifully illustrated late in August 2000 when the Cooleys got a telephone call from the people in Window Rock, Arizona, requesting 2,000 toy cars and trucks for the Navajo Nation's Head Start programs. They were needed before the school year began in early September and time was short

"We had the toys but we didn't have wheels on them," said Charles.

They weren't sure how they were going to meet the deadline until, somehow, a crew at the Rolling Rubber tire shop in Cedar learned about their predicament. Eight of them showed up at the *Happy Factory* one evening and put wheels on 1,000 toys.

"Those guys know their wheels and axles. Thanks to them we were able to deliver the toys on time," Charles says.

People and their needs differed dramatically but all had one thing in common: the heart warming response to a simple wooden toy.

* * * * *

In 2000, Linda Lohrengel, a vision consultant in the Parent Infant Program of the Utah Schools for the Deaf and the Blind (USDB), was driving 500 miles a week as an "itinerant teacher" for blind children in four southern Utah counties.

"Most blind children have other disabilities and most of my students were severely handicapped," explains Lohrengel, now retired by multiple sclerosis and living in Cedar City. She felt they could be helped by *Happy Factory* wooden toys, and that summer took a box of 100, supplied by the Cooleys, to USDB headquarters in Ogden, Utah, for 'modification.'

She says "What normally attracts kids are things like shiny bumpers but we had to adapt these vehicles for children with vision problems."

About 35 children are in residence at the Schools and another 45 are day students, bused to Ogden. All have special needs which can't be met elsewhere, perhaps to learn braille or 'signing' or living skills unavailable in their home territory. But the USDB's main business takes place away from headquarters. Since about two out of every 1,000 children in Utah (and the United States) are blind and around four out of 1,000 are deaf, the major effort is on serving 1,500 deaf and blind children state-wide who live at home and attend regular public schools by running a pre-school program in which specialists such as Lohrengel make home visits to help parents and their deaf or blind children.

"When you can't see what other people do, you can't copy them," explains Judi Neilson, Director of the Parent Infant program which deals with visually-impaired children from birth to three. "Consider how different a little toy car is from a full-size one in which the child rides. Both are cars but getting the different concept across to a child who can't see is difficult."

This problem was overcome to some degree by the unique modifications made to *Happy Factory* vehicles.

"We asked volunteers to use their imaginations and customize the cars and trucks for kids who couldn't see at all or very well," says Marcia Knorr, Alternative Resource Coordinator at USDB, emphasizing that the objective was to create a learning tool, not a beautiful toy, and encouraging them to rifle through their mother's 'junk drawer' for usable materials.

The volunteers responded enthusiastically and well. The toy vehicles were modified with various additions that could be felt, beeped and moved by little fingers. Textures were created with scraps of sandpaper and fabric. Fuzzy balls were glued on headlights. Tiny bells and pipe cleaners were attached. Small magnets were put on the front of two trucks.

"There aren't many adaptive, tactile toys on the market and each modified toy was given to a child to keep," Knorr adds.

At one of the Blind Parent Infant Program's annual family camps, older brothers and sisters modified *Happy Factory* toys in much the same way for a visually-impaired sibling. Barbara Peterson, a visual consultant like Lohrengel, says "It was fun to see their reaction. For blind children, all toy cars usually feel the same and they were much more eager to explore the ones modified by their brother or sister."

A *Happy Factory* steam shovel, delivered later to the school, was as big a hit among the visually-impaired children as those with normal sight. It did not take them long to feel what it was and figure out what it was supposed to do in their sand box, and soon they were competing for a turn sitting on the cab, pushing and pulling the two handles, filling and emptying the scoop.

* * * * *

Not long after the "customization program" got underway in Ogden, the Cooleys received a telephone call from Janeen Holmes, Executive Director of the non-profit Dr. Laura Schlessinger Foundation in Westlake Village, California, who had heard about *The Happy Factory,* and asked for help.

Two years earlier, the nationally-known talk radio hostess and strong advocate of abused and neglected children had asked her12 million listeners what these children most needed. The response pinpointed a major problem: children are often rescued so suddenly that they end up in crisis centers with nothing but the clothes on their back, or lugging a few possessions in trash bags which inspired the dreadful nickname "trash bag kids."

Dr. Laura learned that nearly 300,000 children go into crisis centers or foster homes in the U.S. every year, more often than not empty-handed, with nothing to call their own. So she conceived 'My Stuff' bags, 10 inch by 19 inch duffle bags containing eight or nine items, each new, non-violent and non-denominational. Always included are a blanket, often hand-made, stuffed animal and toiletries. Additional 'stuff' can be such things as a cap, thermos, coloring book, crayons, frisbee, games and costume jewelry.

Volunteers at California headquarters fill the bags, mostly with items donated by listeners, sponsors and corporations, and the implicit as well as explicit message for the child who gets one is that 'lots of people care about you and have given you what's in this bag.'

"In a move, the My Stuff bag goes with the child," explains Holmes.

The Foundation formed in 1998 began operations in her home before finally ending up in the office-warehouse built by Dr. Laura who covers basic overhead including salaries for a staff of seven.

Holmes adds that "We get all kinds of volunteer help. A lot of kids come to do their community service hours - and keep coming back after completing this obligation. Thirty deaf students were here once for three or four hours stuffing bags."

By 2003, the Foundation was serving 736 crisis centers and foster homes nation-wide and the cumulative total had reached 73,000 My Stuff bags.

The hook-up with the Cooleys was a natural and *The Happy Factory* became one of the most regular and reliable donors, starting with delivery of a box of 100 wooden cars and trucks in response to Janeen Holmes' first phone call. They cannot supply a toy for every bag but, almost every month since December 2000, a box or two or sometimes three and four boxes have been shipped to Westlake Village - more than 13,000 by the end of 2003.

Most of the children who get a *Happy Factory* toy or truck realize they are special, hand-made with loving care by volunteers, and that makes the child feel special. In a thank-you letter to Dr. Laura, a young boy wrote "I'm in a bad situation right now and it's a relief to know that someone actually cares."

* * * * *

Somehow or other, although they were not sure exactly why, the Cooley's reach never exceeded their grasp and at times the unexpected became almost normal.

On October 5th, 1999, Donna got a phone call from Mary Ellen Edmunds on the General Board of the LDS Relief Society, seeking the Cooley's support for a special project the following spring. On April 26, 2000, over 10,000 women were expected to attend the annual Women's Conference scheduled to take place in the Brigham Young University football stadium in Provo, Utah. The organizers had decided that painting and distributing several thousand *Happy Factory* toys would be a worthy project, and the Cooleys enthusiastically agreed.

Even with seven months advance notice, the Cedar City *Happy Factory* was hard pushed to fill such a large order but 90 boxes, each holding 100 branded cars and trucks, were in the stadium the following April when the ladies trooped in, picked up their brushes and began to paint. By the time they were done, all 9,000 had been painted and packed back in boxes. A few weeks later, the boxes had been delivered to crisis centers, orphanages, shelters and other organizations serving needy children in Mexico, Peru, Romania and Russia as well as the United States.

Donna reports that "We have had many phone calls requesting toys because of that Women's Conference. And the women all said what a wonderful experience it was."

* * * * *

Shortly before Christmas in 2003, children at the Many Farms, Arizona, boarding school on the Navajo Reservation were in an advanced state of excitement and expectation for the party planned that day. A Christmas stocking had been filled for each of them with several things including candy and a *Happy Factory* car or truck.

That afternoon, as the children started to line up to get their Christmas stocking, a small boy entered the boarding school. No one knew him but the teachers put him in line with the rest of the children. After receiving a stocking, he walked part way across the room before stopping to peek inside. He pulled out a little notebook, looked it over, and dropped it on the floor. Then he pulled out a candy chew, unwrapped it, put the candy in his mouth and dropped the wrapper on the floor. The next item he pulled out of the stocking was a toy truck. He looked and looked at that truck, then walked to an empty corner in the room and began playing with it.

After three hours, he was still playing with his *Happy Factory* truck, oblivious to the party going on around him and ignoring whatever else was in his stocking.

"We have no idea the effect that a small act of kindness might mean to the recipient," says Donna.

* * * * *

Over the years, many other calls for help were not only heard but met. As more needy and needs were identified, *Happy Factory* output steadily increased, from 7,665 toys in 1998 to 17,748 in 1999, 53,167 in 2000, 72,449 in 2001, 62,189 in 2002, 67,734 in 2003 and 107,803 in 2004. At that point, the grand total had reached 388,755, including 808 steam shovels, and was headed still higher, while more than 600 different organizations, groups and people in over 180 countries had received a box or two of toys, or many boxes, depending on their needs.

"That's what this community is all about. We don't have millions of dollars to give away but we have heart and willingness," says Ed Kociela

"This is not a [Latter Day Saints] Ward effort. It's a world effort, and we together are definitely making a drop in a very large bucket," adds Donna, pointing to the *Happy Factory* motto on the wall:

'We may not be able to make a toy for every child in the world who needs one but we're going to try.'

The Happy Factory - Ordinary people doing extraordinary things

Chapter 8 - Steam shovel therapy

Anyone who doubts whether a steam shovel can be therapeutic has never encountered the toy model made in *The Happy Factory*.
This wooden miniature stands 14 inches high with a scoop shovel or bucket on the end of an arm that extends 38 inches out, and moves up or down. The cab swivels on a pipe and giant steel washer atop a sturdy base and provides a seat for the operator (usually, but not always, a child) who can raise, lower, extend, retract, fill or empty the bucket by pulling on two handles. (See illustration).

To be honest, however, therapy was not on Charles Cooley's mind in the spring of 1995 when he was browsing in an Eagle Hardware store in Salt Lake City, on the lookout for interesting toy patterns. Near the exit was a book display and, when he began flipping through 'The Family Handyman - Toys, Games and Furniture' published by the Reader's Digest book department, he spotted a photograph of a little girl sitting on a toy wooden steam shovel.

"At the time, I didn't know where to start and wasn't about to tackle anything that difficult so I bought the book and the steam shovel plans in it and set them aside for two years while I gained more experience working with wood and gained more self-confidence," Charles says. He adds, incidentally, that he's tried ever since to get another copy of the book and never could find one.

Early in the summer of 1997, flush with victory over the Conestoga wagon project, he was primed for a new challenge. Daughter Kris was running the child care center for Cedar City's Shakespearean Festival and he decided to make a steam shovel for the playroom and yard there. The design was well-engineered but a multitude of parts had to be cut out and precise drilling of the holes for a variety of bolts was critical. In fact, it took so long to complete the first one that, computing his time at $15 an hour, he referred to it jokingly thereafter as "a $32,000 steam shovel." But one way and another he got it done and delivered in time for the Festival.

It was a smash hit, overshadowing Shakespeare in the eyes of the younger set. So many kids lined up to use the steam shovel and loved it so much that he decided to build a second one. Number Two went much faster but demand still outran supply. Even with two in operation, the kids were still lining up all day long for a chance to move that bucket up, down and around, and Kris had to use a kitchen timer to limit their turns to eight minutes.

"Several people who saw the steam shovels at the Festival wanted one so I made eleven and sold them for $300 apiece. The money really helped to buy materials and equipment but I didn't want to be in the toy steam shovel business," says Charles.

However, the enthusiasm they generated at the Festival was contagious and, for their next trip to Salt Lake City, the Cooleys made and delivered two *Happy Factory* steam shovels. One went to Primary Children's Medical Center where they immediately got an order for three more. The other went to the Shriners hospital where occupational therapist Kristi Kyte later reported that she had a hard time getting kids back on the treadmill but couldn't keep them off the steam shovel and asked if she could have a second one.

Additional steam shovels were fitted into *The Happy Factory* production schedule and, in due course, were made and delivered. However, Charles and Donna still had no plans to get into the toy steam shovel business.

Then, in December 2000, while visiting friends Kirk and Melinda Brey in Salt Lake City, they mentioned the positive response given *The Happy Factory* steam shovels at the two hospitals. Melissa's sister-in-law worked for Jordan Valley School and they left a steam shovel with the Breys for delivery to the school. This center-based school in Salt Lake City, open

12 months a year, offers 461 severely-disabled children concentrated services delivered by special education teachers and experts in physical, speech, occupational, musical and other kinds of therapy.

When John Gardner, the school principal, called the Cooleys in Cedar City to thank them, he asked if it would be possible to receive three more, explaining "That *Happy Factory* steam shovel caused more chaos than anything I've ever seen, and it was beautiful chaos."

On January 9th, the Cooleys delivered three steam shovels and 50 toy cars and trucks and got a tour of the facilities. *The Happy Factory* toys were a special Christmas present for Gardner, and serendipity was again at work. A week before Christmas, 26 years before, he got a telephone call from the shop teacher at Union High School in Roosevelt, Utah, offering wooden toys made by his students. End result: the Union High-schoolers adopted Jordan Valley School and arrived every December with a fresh batch of toys. In later years, they even made cedar chests and other valuable things which were sold to raise money for what they called their 'secret school.'

"That experience prepared me for *The Happy Factory*," explains Gardner.

What it didn't prepare him for was the impact of miniature steam shovels on his pupils.

Students at Jordan Valley School have at least two primary disabilities and the school, combined with the Child Development Center, serves children almost from birth to age 22. Only 8% are functionally verbal, only 18% are toilet-trained, 26% are fed through G tubes and 53% are in wheel chairs. Many have sound minds trapped in uncooperative bodies and often can 'receive' but can't 'transmit.'

"Our Number One priority is teaching some kind of communicative skills - to smile, blink eyes, point, butt heads against a switch, whatever works. And our second priority is having our kids learn independent living skills," says Gardner. He adds that "We took one steam shovel to the pre-school playroom and every kid wanted to get on it at once. We took another to a classroom of five to seven year old autistic children who were so eager to try it out they couldn't wait for a turn but began pushing each other off."

At the time, of course, neither the Cooleys, Gardner nor Jordan Valley School specialists realized the steam shovels were therapy equipment in disguise, but that soon became clear. It wasn't long before teachers created charts listing students' names and began rewarding them with a star for doing the correct thing when they were asked. So many stars earned them a turn on the steam shovel.

"The little *Happy Factory* cars and trucks were motivational and useful for physical therapy, and children earned playtime with them, but the steam shovels changed their behavior," explains Gardner. He offers two examples.

*A 10 year old boy, in a wheelchair since birth, had only slight control of one hand and one arm. Therapists could tell that he knew where he was and why he was there but he was unable to speak. He was taught how to switch on music or a television set with his 'good' hand but was disinterested, indifferent and withdrawn - until the *Happy Factory* shovels arrived. He spied one and therapists were startled when he became extremely excited, jerking in his wheelchair, smiling and making happy noises. A quick check discovered why. His father was a back hoe operator.

A physical therapist built him an extra seat, with sides and back, that fit on the cab of the toy steam shovel and provided extra support. Since severely disabled children have little muscle because of little opportunity (or inclination) to exercise, therapists worked with him on this modified steam shovel each day, hand in hand, helping him pull one of the two levers. In a few weeks, he could pull the lever unassisted.

Encouraged therapists then attached a lever switch to the arm of his wheelchair. This was linked to a simple computer with a monitor screen showing six square icons, each a symbol with a message - what the experts call Picture Exchange Communications or PECs - such as 'I'm hungry' or 'I'm thirsty' or 'I need to go to the toilet.' He eventually graduated to a computer screen with 32 different icon messages.

"He can now 'talk' to you with the computer. The steam shovel supplied the motivation for him to learn that he could control his 'good' hand," explains Gardner.

* Pre-schoolers at Jordan Valley School, aged two to five, love *The Happy Factory* steam shovels and start playing with them "real early," with therapists sitting beside them and putting their tiny hands on the two levers. One little girl began 'steam shovel therapy' when she was two years old and now, aged five, can operate her own wheel chair outfitted with lever controls.

"When she drives down a hallway in the school all by herself, we all cheer," says Gardner.

For the Cooleys, it was becoming clear that almost anything was do-able, even though some things took longer than others and the world was not always warm smiles and smooth sailing. Witness what happened after they asked Principal Gardner if his school was the only one in Utah for disabled children and had their eyes and hearts opened. They discovered that 49,440 of Utah's 480,000 schoolchildren are "disadvantaged" in one way or another, some major, some minor. The emphasis nowadays is on 'main-streaming' as many of these children as possible into regular neighborhood schools. Some, of course, cannot cope with main-streaming and a special screening committee meets at least weekly to decide who belongs in the state's 57 center-based schools similar to Jordan Valley School.

Moved by the plight of these children, Charles called the Utah State Office of Education (USOE) and was shocked by his chilly reception, unaware that USOE was the favorite target of all kinds of people pursuing their own selfish interests.

"We're deluged with calls and have to be skeptical," explains Karen Buchanan, the secretary and right-hand-woman of Education Specialist Jocelyn Taylor.

Taylor says "I found the Cooley's offer too good to be true and hard to believe. I wondered 'what do they really want?'"

The Cooleys were taken aback. Charles says "The attitude of people there was 'What's in it for you?' and no one was willing to meet with us."

Since their unannounced calls and offers of toys to Primary Children's Medical Center, Shriners hospital, the Humanitarian Center and Jordan Valley School had met with such warm welcomes, neither Charles nor Donna had felt it necessary to ask their 'satisfied customers' to intercede with USOE on their behalf.

Although bewildered, both were confident their *Happy Factory* cars and trucks, and especially steam shovels, had something valuable to offer children. Early in February, ignoring the initial brush-off, they swallowed their pride and Donna telephoned again. This time, her call was put through to Karen Buchanan who did not know about Charles' experience a month earlier and was intrigued by the offer of free *Happy Factory* toys.

She checked with a USOE specialist who snorted "It's just a scam. They want an endorsement."

Even so, Buchanan was undeterred. She figured 'What have we got to lose?' and her boss encouraged her to set up a meeting with the Cooleys.

The initial reaction of four USOE specialists at that meeting was skeptical.

"What's in it for you?" one asked.

However, when he and his associates learned there was no charge for *Happy Factory* steam shovels and saw one demonstrated, their reaction was "wide-eyed and Wow!" according to one of those present.

"I understand you need forty steam shovels, one for each school district," said Charles at the end of his demonstration.

The indifference and disbelief had evaporated and the education specialists hastily explained that they needed 250 steam shovels, not 40, since some districts had more than one school for severely disabled children and many regular schools had special classrooms for disadvantaged children who could be helped by 'steam shovel therapy.'

"I can't promise that many. I'll have to talk with Mel Griguhn," Charles replied, explaining that *The Happy Factory* organization was unique. "There are no bosses. Mel and Frank DelDuca *work* out their own production schedule for steam shovels and 180 are budgeted for 2001."

When Charles told his associates back in Cedar about the Utah State Office of Education request, Mel shrugged. "I'm just cutting up boards. Seems like good job security for me."

Jocelyn Taylor explained later that "When Charles demonstrated that big beautiful hardwood steam shovel, we had to get over our shock that someone was trying to give us something for free, with no strings attached. His spirit of goodness was really obvious and he won me over. I realized this service was a good thing and the steam shovels would benefit our children and asked Karen if she would handle it. It was a real hassle to contact all the school districts but Karen had caught the vision and went at it."

Buchanan emailed and FAXed Special Education Directors in all the Utah school districts and *The Happy Factory* began making regular steam shovel deliveries to the Office of Education headquarters in Salt Lake City, starting with five on February 20th. In succeeding months, Buchanan was up to her elbows in steam shovels at times, struggling to find temporary parking places for them until they were picked up by school district representatives, and she caught flak occasionally from colleagues irritated by the clutter. But she collected smiles as well as she wrestled the boxes into an empty corner or unused office and topped each off with ten *Happy Factory* cars and trucks, and she was often asked if she was 'the toy lady.'

At her request, the Bear, mascot of the Utah Jazz National Basketball Association team, came to USOE headquarters one afternoon to hand over a steam shovel to a grateful Special Education Director.

She says "The positive response was wonderful everywhere. Nobody was negative and *Happy Factory* steam shovels are being used for therapy, as training and learning tools, and for discipline."

It took Mel and Frank two years but, on February 19, 2003, the Cooleys delivered the last of 256 steam shovels to the Office of Education.

Karen Buchanan told them "*Happy Factory* steam shovels are a God-send. They not only teach the children eye-hand coordination but over-all coordination as well."

The Happy Factory had produced as promised, the 'contract' with USOE was fulfilled at no charge, and every school in Utah for disabled children and every classroom with disadvantaged children had at least one steam shovel in operation.

"People can't believe what the Cooleys do," says Jocelyn Taylor.

Unsurprisingly, there have been multiple targets for their steam shovels

Two were first delivered to the Humanitarian Center in May 1998 and, by the following October, a *Happy Factory* steam shovel was being added to each container of clothing, medical supplies, hygiene kits, toys and other things shipped worldwide to those in need . Since then, a steam shovel and two boxes of toys have been put in every 100 pound Children's Institutional Module sent to orphanages, hospitals, clinics and such, and *The Happy Factory* is supplying the Humanitarian Center up to 10 steam shovels each month.

"Can you imagine the value a steam shovel adds to each module?" Rich McKenna, a senior Humanitarian Services official said to Charles one day as he made another delivery.

"Three hundred dollars?" Charles suggested, thinking back to his experience at the Cedar City Shakespearean Festival.

"Oh my no," replied McKenna. "The value to the children can't be measured in dollars and cents. Those steam shovels are priceless."

He explained that, in many Third World countries, there is no money for equipment and no equipment available even if money was. These poor countries have nothing in the therapy departments of their hospitals. Later, Lloyd Pendleton showed the Cooleys a photograph of a little boy on a steam shovel in a hospital in the Republic of Georgia. The only things in the therapy room were the boy, the steam shovel, a green plant and a crack in the wall.

At home and abroad, the heart-warming success stories multiplied.

* During his therapy sessions at Shriners hospital, four year old Riley Lloyd fell in love with his 'digger,' otherwise known as a *Happy Factory* steam shovel. Cerebral palsy had left Riley with little use of his legs but a bit of strength in his arms. Therapists had to set him on the seat but, after that, he worked it with increasing vigor. In November 2000, his mother called the Cooleys to ask if she could buy Riley a steam shovel and how much would it cost.

"You've paid the price," replied Donna. "We would be happy to deliver a steam shovel to your home at no cost."

They did so and, says Charles, "We wish everyone could have seen the smile on Riley's face when he saw it and, especially, when his mom placed him on it and his arms immediately started to work those levers."

* Two year old Daniel, born without a right hand and with part of his right arm missing, was fitted with a prosthetic substitute at Shriners. With this artificial 'helper' in place and his left hand, he could work the steam shovel and wore a broad smile. His parents asked Kristi Kyte if there was any way they could buy one to have at their home since it was the only piece of 'rehab equipment' he was willing to use with his 'helper.' Kristi gave them the Cooley's phone number and theirs to the Cooleys.

"We did not hear from them," says Charles, "probably because they didn't know how to ask us for a steam shovel. The father had been laid off, and was looking for work, and they were living in Salt Lake City with his folks. So I called them and explained that we'd be happy to make a steam shovel for Daniel at no cost. His mother was silent for several seconds and I told her she had paid the price. A couple of weeks later, we delivered the steam shovel, a toy lawnmower and a wooden hippo to Daniel at his home. What a beautiful child, shy but so excited. He made our hearts melt."

* Several years ago, the Tiny Tim Foundation (TTF), established and operated by Alton and Cheryl Thacker (see Chapter 6) 'adopted' the school for handicapped children in Ascension, Mexico. It had four rooms, a toilet that was flushed once a day with a bucket, and little else before the TTF supplied and installed such things as handrails on the walls,

carpeting and mirrors six feet wide and three feet high which reflected the attempts of teachers to help students move their limbs. There were no trained therapists and no therapy equipment of any kind.

Early in 2001, while visiting *The Happy Factory* in Cedar, Al asked if he could have a steam shovel for the school.

Charles Cooley said "Of course. That's what they're for. Take one."

In April, on their next trip to Mexico, Al and Cheryl arrived at the school shortly before 9 AM in their Ford 250 diesel truck, pulling a trailer load of gifts for needy people in Ascension, and delivered the steam shovel to Blanca, the principal. They had barely unloaded it when Andres, 10, was pushed into the school in his wheelchair.

He would not or could not use his arms or legs but, when he spotted the new arrival, cried "I want to run the steam shovel!"

"You can't because you can't use your hands or feet," replied Blanca.

"I will if you put me on it," said Andres.

This is a short version of the sharp interchange in Spanish which Blanca later translated for the Thackers. Andres was pushed into his classroom, the steam shovel was left as the only piece of therapy equipment in the school, and the Thackers returned home.

Six weeks later, they drove back to Ascension with another trailer load of gifts and stopped by the school. The children knew they were coming and, when he heard the truck, Andres pleaded with Blanca to put him on the steam shovel.

"Quick, quick!" he cried.

When the Thackers walked into the classroom, he was grinning from ear to ear and showing off his ability.

"He could make that steam shovel do anything he wanted and of course we bragged on him," said Al Thacker.

That Christmas, back in Ascension with more gifts, the Thackers were pleasantly shocked to find Andres had discarded his wheelchair and was getting to school by himself with the help of a three-wheeled walker. When they returned in April 2002, a year after delivering the steam shovel, they naturally asked "Where's Andres?"

"Oh, Andres is gone," replied Blanca.

Their concern was so obvious that she hurriedly added "He's graduated from the handicapped school. He runs now and can catch the ball when the children play."

Blanca and the Thackers are convinced that *The Happy Factory* steam shovel provided the motivation Andres needed to strengthen his arms and legs and graduate from his wheelchair to a walker and then to walk and run.

* Mel Griguhn's granddaughter, 8 year old Katie, is in Stacie Rasmussen's class at Fiddler's Elementary School in Cedar City which was preparing a report on occupations. Katie brought her grandfather to school and, when he spotted 8 year old Tony, she explained that her classmate was disabled. He had been kept in the hospital for more than a year after he was born prematurely and had learned to walk but had difficulty speaking and holding a pencil. Tony was 'main-streamed' into Fiddler's and is attended by an aide, Annette Jackson.

The next day, back at *The Happy Factory,* Mel told the Cooleys about his visit to Fiddler's Elementary and said "There's a little boy in Katie's class who could use a *Happy Factory* steam shovel. Could I take him one?"

"Of course," said Charles.

Soon after that, Donna improved on the basic plan with a telephone call, offering a small *Happy Factory* vehicle for each child in the class, plus a steam shovel for Tony.

"That's a wonderful idea," said Stacie.

She checked with Tony's parents, who were delighted, and on a sunny morning in May, the Cooleys delivered 27 unpainted cars and trucks, paint, brushes and a steam shovel to Fiddler's Elementary School.

"We had a ball and Tony was thrilled," says Stacie, explaining that all 27 kids painted for thirty minutes, then Tony got on the steam shovel and became so absorbed that he skipped recess. "Everyone had a turn on the steam shovel but, what the kids enjoyed most, was watching Tony manipulate the controls. His classmates really care. They sense that he is different and protect him on the playground. And that steam shovel was therapeutic. By the end of the day, he was using both levers to work it."

The whole class collaborated with Stacie on the following note, dated May 20, 2003:

"Dear Happy Factory,
  Thank you for the cars. We had fun painting them. Thank you for letting Tony have the big steam shovel. He loves it! He let us all have a turn. The cars are beautiful. We are excited to show our moms and dads. Thank you for working hard to make children happy. You are so nice.

It was poster size, signed by all the children, and hangs proudly on the HF wall.

Stacie reports: "By the end of the school year, Tony could read, work math problems and speak. I cried when he left. He misses school and wants to come back. Next year he will be in Grade 3 and may be main-streamed until he's 21."

She talked with Tony's parents the other day. Both are students, attending school and working. They report that the neighborhood kids come over to play regularly and his younger brother gets a turn on the steam shovel.

The Happy Factory steam shovels have become quite a story. Demand remains strong and, as of December 31, 2004, 808 have been delivered. These include a 'special delivery' to the City of Hope Hospital in Duarte, California, by Tom Smith, a regular volunteer in the Cedar City *Happy Factory*, as well as a delivery to the Northern California Shriners Hospital and a 500 bed hospital in El Salvador.

Jordan Valley School Principal John Gardner sums up the reaction everywhere in two sentences. "What really surprised us was that *Happy Factory* steam shovels are far more than a fun toy. They ended up as therapy equipment."

Definitely not a scrap pile Charles is checki

Making a steam shovel takes extra time and patience

It's fussy and finicky work but satisfying

Steam Shovel Therapy

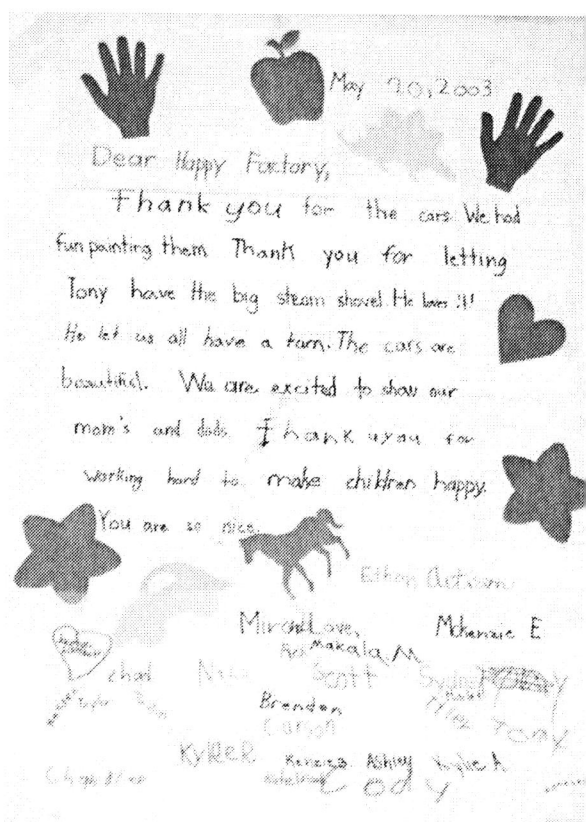

(above) Riley Lloyd masters his steam shovel

(right) A letter from grade 2, Chandler's Elementary School

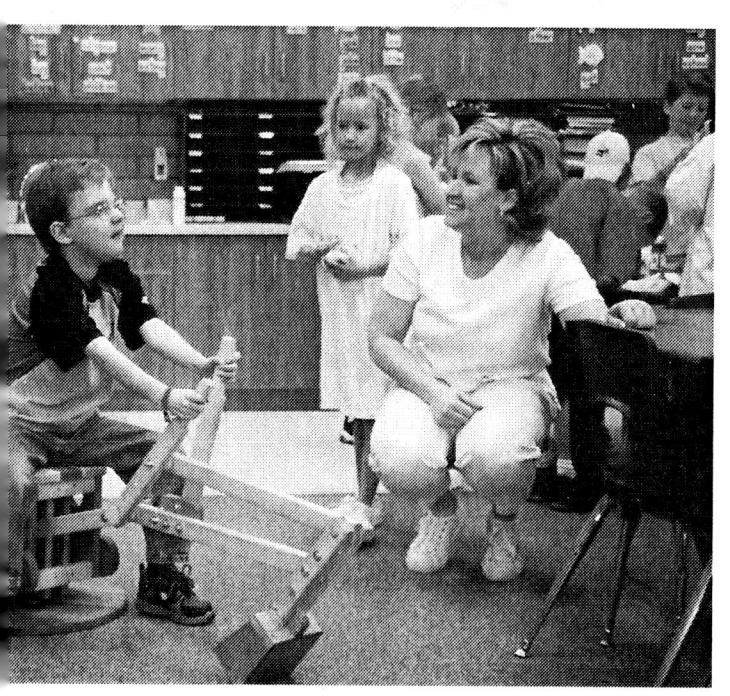

(left) Riley shows classmates how his steam shovel works.

The Happy Factory - Ordinary people doing extraordinary things

Chapter 9 - Uncommon helpers

The Happy Factory is a generosity generator. All kinds of people volunteer and do what they do because the return, measured in satisfaction rather than money, is so superb. Some are uncommon helpers because of the unique nature of what they've done or how they've done it or what they're still doing. For example:

* * * * *

Never underestimate a happenstance. In the summer of 1996, Thurl Bailey, a star player for the National Basketball Association's Utah Jazz team, was conducting a basketball camp for youths in Hurricane, Utah, 40 miles south of Cedar City. Helping out was Jon Absey, the team's Special Events Coordinator who schedules appearances of the Jazz Bear, the team mascot. When Charles Cooley heard about the camp, he instinctively recognized potential assets for *The Happy Factory* were at hand so he and Paul Cozzens stopped by, found their way through bouncing balls and a clutter of sweating young males, and introduced themselves to Bailey and Absey.

It was a meeting of kindred spirits and the beginning of beautiful friendships. En route home to Salt Lake City after the basketball camp ended, Absey and Bailey visited the original *Happy Factory* in the shed behind the Cooley house to learn more about the operation. Both men were hooked and eventually joined the Board of Trustees.

"*The Happy Factory* toys were infectious and so were the Cooleys, "says Bailey.

"What *The Happy Factory* does strictly for kids, with volunteers contributing their time and energy and nobody making a dime, is so unselfish in this day and age that it's almost unheard of," adds Absey.

That same year, a few weeks before Christmas, the Cooleys

readily fulfilled Absey's request for a box of toy cars and trucks for the Jazz Bear to hand out at Primary Children's Medical Center and Shriners Hospital, and this has become a Christmas tradition. A Hallowe'en handout was added later to the Bear's schedule.

"Charles is on the ball. He calls me every October and December to ask if the Bear needs toys, then drives up from Cedar and delivers them to the Delta Center [home of the Utah Jazz and the Bear]," reports Absey.

The Jazz Bear was created in 1994 to add a dash of entertainment value to home games and help generate favorable publicity for the team. Absey joined the organization the same year to handle the mascot's activities.

He says "The Bear's main focus is on kids. He makes three to four appearances daily, seven days a week, during the basketball season, and three to four weekly the rest of the year."

This goodwill ambassador has become a popular entertainer in Utah, appearing at 'grand openings,' school assemblies, the Neighborhood House, Primary Children's, Ronald McDonald House, School of No Name, Shriners hospital, Marshal White Center and other worthy targets, and he takes needy kids Back to School shopping and Christmas shopping as well.

"The Bear could hand out *Happy Factory* toys at every appearance but, if he did, they would not always go to under-privileged children and would lose their meaning and purpose," says Absey. Just in case, however, a bag of 'spare' *Happy Factory* cars and trucks is normally kept in the support van for times when the Bear spots a deserving child in the audience who could use a toy.

Absey adds: "A *Happy Factory* toy is better than a Jazz token. Everyone ends up on the floor playing with them."

The Bear has appeared at several *Happy Factory* fund raisers, including the first one, a celebrity basketball game and concert in Cedar City organized by Thurl Bailey on September 20, 1999. Earlier that day, the gang from Salt Lake City all gathered at *The Happy Factory* for a look-learn- and-work session.

"We couldn't get the Bear away from the band saw," says Donna Cooley. "He spent two and a half hours sawing away and told me it was neat to know that a toy he cut out might end up in China or Romania making some child happy."

Thurl Bailey and his Family Entertainment Foundation followed up the celebrity basketball game with several more *Happy Factory* fund raisers, including the August 2003, gala dinner in Cedar. Bailey, now an ex-NBA player and Jazz TV commentator, polished Master of Ceremonies and professional singer, delighted his audience at that show and helped raise almost $28,000 for the *Happy Factory* building fund.

* * * * *

On a frigid January morning in 2000 when Charles Cooley picked up the mail in his Cedar City post office box, he noticed a small envelope neatly addressed to *The Happy Factory* with a Tooele, Utah, street and number in the upper left corner as a return address but no name.

Curiosity aroused, he opened the envelope and found two one-dollar bills inside, paper-clipped to a small yellow memo sheet. On the sheet, undated and unsigned, someone had written 'This is all I can do. I hope it will help.'

Charles says "When my vision cleared, I put the money back in the envelope and thought to myself 'It costs us 40 cents to make a toy. That's 2 1/2 toys for a dollar and five for two dollars. There are five children somewhere in the world who think it helped a lot.'"

A year later, the Cooleys were in Tooele with a *Happy Factory* steam shovel for Riley Lloyd, the young boy stricken with cerebral palsy. After making that delivery, they drove to the street address of the Anonymous Donor of the two dollars. Set back from the sidewalk was a small, old but well-kept house with dolls, doilies and other hand-crafts displayed For Sale on the porch.

They knocked on the front door and an older lady opened it.

"Could you be our Anonymous Donor?" asked Donna with a sweet smile.

Donna says it was difficult to describe the look on the lady's face. "She knew we'd found her but was not over-anxious to be identified. We thanked her again for the donation, gave her a hug and left. And we still don't know her name."

* * * * *

There must be something special about the power of two dollars for *The Happy Factory*.

In early December 2003, Charles met with a youth group in Cedar to talk about giving service and *The Happy Factory*. At the end of his presentation, he asked for questions and a boy about 14 years old raised his hand.

"How do you donate to *The Happy Factory*?" he asked.

"Please see me at the end of the meeting," Charles replied.

They met in a quiet corner. Charles explained that donations were gladly accepted at any time and handed the boy his *Happy Factory* name card.

"Would right now be alright?" the boy asked.

Charles nodded okay. The boy carefully extracted two one dollar bills from his wallet, handed them over and said apologetically "Sorry, but that's all I have."

Charles had vision problems again but managed to say "That's just fine. Your two dollars will cover the cost of five *Happy Factory* toys and make five children happy somewhere in the world."

* * * * *

Eric Lee, 16, needed an Eagle Scout project and knew exactly where to turn. He telephoned his grandparents, Charles and Donna Cooley, and his timing could not have been better.

That call was placed late in 2001 after the Cooleys had received a request from Drs. Ernie and Elaine Weeks for 500 bags of wooden blocks, each holding 24 pieces, for their A Basketful of Child Development (ABCD) program in Paraguay. (see Chapter 10)

The Weeks had contacted the Cooleys again because *The Happy Factory's* unofficial rules had been severely bent out of shape twice before to make blocks - for them to take to Haiti and for their colleague, Utah State University Professor Anne Austin, to put in Paraguay's first Learning Baskets. The

Cooleys couldn't say No and both requests had been cheerfully filled, but block-making is not what *The Happy Factory* was designed to do and twice was enough.

"We were in the toy business. We weren't interested in such a time-consuming process as more block-making," explains Charles.

Fortunately for the Weeks, however, their request was a perfect fit for Eric's purposes since projects that met Eagle Scout standards were hard to find.

"I needed a good size project. It was just what I wanted," he says.

He immediately began planning and organizing and was surprised not only by how long it took to work out all the details, large and small, but how much time and trouble was involved in getting the volunteer help he needed to make 12,000 blocks.

But, as he points out, "One of the biggest benefits of an Eagle Scout project is learning leadership skills."

He enlisted 8 scouts from his troop in Enoch, Utah, and persuaded 10 scouts from another troop to help out. His mother, father and sister agreed to pitch in as well and, in November, production got underway evenings at *The Happy Factory* in Cedar City.

Charles supplied 1½" wide by 3/4" thick milled strips of hardwood and a cutting plan for turning them efficiently into blocks 1½ inches, 3 inches and 6 inches long with minimum waste, and explained that, to do a quality job, the sawed side of each block needed sanding, all edges needed routing and two holes had to be drilled in the 6" blocks to take wooden pegs.

To transform wood strips into 12,000 carefully-sawed, sanded, routed and drilled blocks was a formidable task that took some 200 man- and woman-hours, including the 35 hours Eric spent in planning, securing and scheduling his work force, and managing production and final inspection.

"The hardest part was finding people to help but things went pretty smoothly. My family and most of my friends cooperated," says Eric who was especially grateful to have the *Happy Factory*, with its wood-working machinery, as a work place. "We were excited to do this for little kids. It helps you not just to think about yourself and makes you realize how lucky you are. It was pretty cool."

Early in December, he and his father loaded the family car with 12,000 blocks, all finished professionally and neatly bagged, and drove 250 miles north through a snowstorm to deliver them to the Humanitarian Center in Salt Lake City.

His reward was a good deal more than satisfaction with a job well done. A few months later, a packet of photographs arrived, showing Paraguayan children playing with the blocks and other contents of the Learning Baskets.

"Those pictures were far more than I was expecting," says a beaming Eric.

* * * * *

Steve Mills is a barn builder and a *Happy Factory* donor and that's not all. Fortunately for Al Thacker and two Mexican communities, he has designed and engineered other buildings as well.

After working for nine years developing new products and expanding sales for another barn builder, Mills was startled one day to have his employer complain that he'd never wanted his company to grow so big. Result: in 1994, Mills started his own business, S&S Barns and Buildings, in a Salt Lake City suburb with a silent partner in Las Vegas.

Initially, S&S built conventional buildings with pipe frames and galvanized steel walls. In 2000, however, Mills began to diversify, welding 1½" galvanized steel pipe into frames for walls and roofs, clad by colored steel panels three feet wide, fastened on the frames with self-tapping tech screws, and pierced by windows and doors wherever necessary.

"My design has not been successfully copied yet and has evolved. By reinforcing the steel pipe trusses, we can construct buildings with clear spans up to 36 feet," he explains.

No concrete foundation is necessary for these unique S&S buildings. They can be any length, are normally one story high, and can be put together with a 9/16" wrench and an electric drill. The big advantage, aside from savings of 20% over wooden structures, is portability.

He says "They can be taken apart in sections, with sheathing and insulation in place, and moved to a new site on a flat bed truck."

S&S now has at least one dealer in every state west of Colorado and ships to Hawaii, Florida and Mexico. Although 95% of the business is barns, the product line-up has expanded to sheds, garages, storage buildings and other special function structures.

Early in 2001, Mills met Al Thacker who needed a sturdy building in Colonial Juarez, Mexico, to replace the tired old apple shed in which Tiny Tim Foundation (TTF) volunteers were assembling wheelchairs donated by Americans.

Says Thacker "Steve wanted to give us a building and asked what we needed. I gave him the dimensions of the apple shed and that's what we got."

"That building was a miracle and one of the best experiences I've ever had," adds Mills.

Impressed by TTF's good deeds, he offered to donate the 50 foot x 65 foot building and the labor to erect it - namely himself, his brother and three friends from Salt Lake City plus his partner and four other men from Las Vegas. Only one of the 10 men - Mills - had any experience in construction and all were due back at work in a week.

Around noon Tuesday, June 5, their caravan - a large flat bed truck loaded with the building in parts and the volunteers in a motor home and pickup trucks - reached the Columbus, New Mexico, border crossing and were stopped cold on the Mexican side by Customs officers in Palomas who shrugged aside any and all explanations about the charitable nature of the mission and demanded "mordida." [literally a bite, but better-known as a bribe.] For the next two and a half days the Americans sat at the border crossing, frustrated, fuming and telephoning frantically to anyone in either country who might be able to help. Nothing worked. No bribes, no budge.

Mills was desperate. His crew was becoming hostile and wanted to head home. Finally, a contact in Colonial Juarez called to say a certain Mexican Customs officer at the El Paso-Juarez border 90 miles to the east, would let them cross. When they got there Friday evening, however, their man had left for the weekend. Baffled and defeated, the Americans prepared to head north when an old Volkswagen rattled up. Their contact, who had returned for a forgotten coat, spotted the caravan, signed the necessary papers and passed them into Mexico.

"That was the first miracle," says Mills.

They arrived in Colonial Juarez at 10 PM Friday night and were relieved to find the dirt pad for the new building level and ready. But there was another big problem. All 10 men were due back at their jobs in the United States on Tuesday morning. Only two working days were left, not the five days Mills had figured as the bare minimum needed to get two-thirds of the building up, enough to show locals how to finish it.

At 6 AM Saturday, they began building. By noon, despite 105oF heat and no shade, most of the frame was up. By 9 PM, with brief stops for lunch and dinner, the frame was completely finished and both sides were sheathed. Work resumed Sunday at 6 AM and, by 6 PM, the building was done, roof on, walls in place, weather-tight.

"That was the second miracle. Everything went together perfectly. Nothing was missing. There wasn't a single problem," says Mills.

He was understandably proud of his design but that wasn't the answer on this job. "My best crew in Salt Lake would have taken four days and my dysfunctional crew did it in two. We had Help!" he adds, looking heaven-ward. They had done the impossible.

Early Monday morning, the men shook hands, said "When are we coming back?" and then drove all day and all night to get back to their regular jobs Tuesday morning.

The next summer, Thacker called Mills about erecting a *Happy Factory* in the yard behind the house he'd swapped for a condo so he could make more toys for needy children.

"I was excited by his objective. It's unbelievable what he and the Tiny Tim Foundation do, so I donated the building and helped him and his volunteers put it together," says Mills, adding a $16,000 gift to the $68,000 structure erected in Colonial Juarez the year before.

Thacker's *Happy Factory* #19, up and running in September 2002, was followed by a 60 foot by 60 foot hospital sponsored by the TTF, donated by Mills, trucked to Ascension, Mexico, and erected in May 2004 by the same ten men from Salt Lake City and Las Vegas plus one of Mill's key men from S&S who went along to add muscle and moxie in case they ran short of miracles.

* * * * *

Not many 43 year old college graduates seeking a Master's degree in Business Administration would devote an entire summer without pay as a sweat laborer in a *Happy Factory*. But that's exactly what Gary Hyatt decided to do and he got there in 2003 by a tortuous route.

Hyatt is a veteran grocer. At age 16, while attending high school in Las Vegas, he began to learn the grocery business working part-time for Smith's Food and Drug Stores. Later, at Brigham Young University (BYU) in Provo, Utah, while getting a Bachelor's degree in Business Management, the special education continued.

"It took me six years to get a four year degree because I got married in 1981 and began working 40 hours a week at Smith's as close-up manager, locking the doors at midnight, as well as attending school," says Hyatt.

After graduating in 1986, he moved to Washington State to work as an intern in Safeway Store's management training program. In autumn 1987, he was promoted to Assistant Manager and, for the next 13 years, moved from store to store in the Seattle metropolitan area, finding each job presented new challenges.

"People skills are the most important for people in retail. You must learn how to deal effectively with employees and customers," says Hyatt.

The move in 1991 to a south Seattle store in the heart of a black ghetto as a trouble-shooter put those skills to work with a vengeance.

"Every store is different and bullets were flying on more than one occasion in this one. Bold shoplifters would try to hide a large roast inside their pants or skirts, and cashiers sometimes openly skimmed money from the till. It was a high stress store with a high burn-out rate for managers, but it was fun," Hyatt explains.

He and the manager worked well as a team and, among other actions, were forced to terminate several employees. This did not make them popular but, since the manager was black, Hyatt who is white bore the brunt of staff resentment. Six months after moving on to manage a smaller store in west Seattle, he was startled by a demotion, the result of bad evaluations from several disgruntled employees in the ghetto store.

Hyatt decided he had three choices: quit, or loaf along and do just enough to get by until retirement at 55, or prove his tormentors wrong. He took the latter tack and, 18 months later, was re-evaluated and promoted back to manager. Although more promotions to ever bigger stores followed, the grocery business had begun to pall.

He says "By June 2001, I felt the company and I were going down different paths. It took a loyal wife and a lot of prayer to quit Safeway, but I hated the job and didn't like the kind of person it was making me - tired, stressed out and on edge all the time. Most Safeway managers retire at 55, burned out. They've had enough."

The search for a new job convinced him a Master's degree was desirable and he decided to go back to BYU. After working part-time at Safeway, he sold the house in August 2002 and headed for Provo with wife Shannon, three sons and three daughters.

The Happy Factory entered his life indirectly the following spring when Charles and Donna Cooley were speakers at the annual women's conference at BYU attended by Shannon Hyatt. A few weeks later, Gary started a summer job with a small Provo company but left after six days because the owner was dishonest and wanted Hyatt to be dishonest as well.

The Cooleys and their hand-made wooden toys had impressed both Hyatts and, says Gary, "Two things sent me to work in a *Happy Factory*. I needed something to keep me busy, and something to keep me out of my wife's hair."

Al Thacker's *Happy Factory*, a 40 minute, 30 mile commute

north to Sandy, Utah, was the closest and handiest one and, on May 19th, 2003, Hyatt began working there six to seven hours a day, five days a week.

Thacker, perennially short-handed, could hardly believe his good fortune. He'd never had a full-time helper and Hyatt was willing to do whatever was needed most - glue, trace, saw, drill, sand, rout or brand. Before long, the Sandy factory was turning out 1,000 cars and trucks each week.

"Gary was a God-send," says Thacker. "I was looking down the barrel for shoulder surgery and four months working with one arm. Gary has a curious mind and likes to find out how things work. He hadn't been here a month and he could run everything   He's good with people and before long was conducting tours and doing it all."

Asked how he could stand the boring, repetitive work, Hyatt shrugs. "I made a commitment and did what I could. It's a great cause and I was there to work. It was a relaxing, stress-less, undemanding job and you could think about anything you wanted."

He never missed a day before returning to BYU in late August to resume his studies, with emphasis on the corporate supply chain track.

After Hyatt left with a smile and a hearty one-arm hug from Al, there was unexpected fall-out from his selfless summer work. On a field trip to Chicago, classmates in the MBA Marketing Club at the university delivered 500 cars and trucks from the Thackers to a children's hospital. And Jim Stice, Director of the BYU MBA program, decided to have his marketing and finance graduate students devise a fund-raising program to relieve Al Thacker from the chore he dreaded the most - raising money.

* * * *

Every day. Nola Phillips has problems, hundreds of them, all men.

Phillips is Deputy Warden at Utah State Prison's Lone Peak facility a few miles south of Salt Lake City which is home to some 400 inmates, all males with less than three years left on their sentences before parole. Many serve in crews, under supervision, on a variety of jobs outside the prison, from asbestos abatement and construction to cleaning up roads and sealing cracks in highway pavement. Even so, Phillips felt all were left with too much idle time on their hands.

So in October 2003, when she decided some kind of humanitarian service would be good for them, Phillips talked it over with her daughter who suggested checking out the Thacker's *Happy Factory* in Sandy. Intrigued by what she was told on the telephone about how toy wooden cars and trucks were made and given away, she stopped by their factory the next day, talked with Cheryl Thacker and came away with 180 toys that needed a paint job.

Back at the prison, several inmates were as impressed as she was about what was done in *Happy Factory #19*. Equipped with paint, brushes and patience, they had 180 of the toy cars and trucks beautifully painted within two days..

On her second trip to the Sandy factory, Phillips delivered the 180 painted toys and picked up 300 more bare wood cars and trucks, plus 100 which required a re-do after other painters botched the job. All were meticulously painted or re-painted and returned a week later to *Happy Factory #19* and exchanged for 1,000 in need of tender, loving care at the Lone Peak facility where painting toy cars and trucks had suddenly become the in-thing to do.

A multi-purpose room 12 foot x 24 foot was made available 12 hours a day, seven days a week, for some 60 avid painters, and two inmate workers were paid 40 cents an hour as monitors. Some inmates were soon painting all day, every day. Others picked up a brush after work. And they quickly established a five step production routine.

Each *Happy Factory* car or truck was given an additional fine grit sanding, then a base coat of paint. This was followed by carefully-painted trim - windows, head lights and tail lights - before a team of three specialists added imaginative details. Then wheels were hammered on. Everyone was on the same wave length, so occupied and preoccupied with toy production that there were no trouble-makers and no problems.

In six weeks, the Lone Peak painters finished nearly 1,600

Happy Factory cars and trucks and, on December 11th, 1,047 samples of their handiwork were neatly parked in the prison gymnasium, on the floor and on two long tables near a third table covered with 250 colorful hats crocheted for needy children from donated yarn by inmates, many of whom were painters as well.

"Painting is a privilege, and it keeps them busy," says Phillips, who maintains discipline over her charges with a firm but fair hand. "They're all volunteers and some guys paint 12 hours a day."

Why do they bother? It's a labor of love, and their attitude is as heartwarming as their output.

One inmate explains: "One thousand and forty-seven toy cars equal one thousand and forty-seven happy children."

Another says: "We grew up better than the kids who get these toys so if we give back and produce a smile, we do a good job."

A third declares: "Obviously I haven't been a good boy or I wouldn't be here. Painting cars makes me feel good about myself."

The inmates, who live in 50-man dormitories fitted with double bunks, are almost all inside Lone Peak prison instead of outside because of a drug problem.

"When all you can think about is your next fix, you'll do anything to get it - burglary, theft, whatever it takes," explains Phillips, noting sadly that roughly three out of four of her inmates can't kick their drug habit and are back in Lone Peak soon after their release.

Under the circumstances, the painters take special pride in making a contribution to society. Most of the toys finished at Lone Peak are miniature works of art on which an inmate 'finishing specialist' may have labored for an hour or two, so exquisitely painted that a visiting crew from TV Channel 13 in Salt Lake City found it difficult to decide what to ignore and what to shoot for the 9 o'clock news program that night.

The December 11th display in the prison gymnasium was only a start.

"We'll deliver the 1,047 this afternoon and pick up some

more," promised Deputy Warden Phillips.

* * * * *

An interview published in the October 20, 2003, issue of the Salt Lake Tribune identified Jim Greenbaum as "one of the richest Utahns you've never heard of." That was an apt description of a man who favors philanthropy rather than publicity and quietly gives away more than a million dollars every year.

"My whole goal in life was to make as much money as possible in the shortest possible time so I could spend it helping to make the world a better place," explains Greenbaum who is anything but a misty-eyed, impractical idealist. He considers himself a liberal Republican and compassionate conservative who measures his compassion carefully and selectively. His aim was to become what he calls "a venture philanthropist" and how he got to be one is a tale with several twists and turns.

Greenbaum was born and raised in Louisiana, majored in psychology at the University of Virginia in 1980 and, after working a few summers for a law firm, was two weeks away from entering law school before deciding the practice of law was not for him. Far more appealing was the business world. Several entrepreneurial adventures, including making and selling Hayfever Helmets, (customized head-wear for allergy sufferers), followed and failed yet all of them were part of an invaluable post-grad education, convincing him that the easiest way to make money was by doing something other people were already doing and just doing it better.

The next learning experience was work at a family-owned, long distance telephone service company in Las Vegas, burdened with the wrong equipment, wrong management style and wrong marketing.

Says Greenbaum "The concept was good and I decided, if done the right way, such a company could make a fortune."

A colleague recommended Salt Lake City as a good place for a start-up and, in 1985, after a brief market study, he moved to the Utah capital and founded Access Long Distance, a full service, long distance, telecommunications company. The

AT&T breakup earlier in that decade had opened the market and spawned a multitude of competitors, yet Access was able to compete successfully, head-to-head, with the big companies.

"We offered Cadillac service at Volkswagen prices," explains Greenbaum, emphasizing that their prices were not the lowest but their service was the best.

His company focused on the nine Western states and, 14 years later, had 300 employees and was generating annual revenues of $100 million. The time was right and Access Long Distance was sold for $250 million to McLeod USA which needed a Western U.S. operation and wanted Access employees, system, methods and management. Greenbaum and a partner controlled the company but were not majority owners. Although his partner stayed on with McLeod, Greenbaum had other priorities. He had formed the James R. Greenbaum Foundation in 1993 and was ready to put much of his share of the sale to work in a special way.

"I invest in people with vision and ability who have recently created organizations designed to make the world a better place. It's like investing in a business at the incubation stage," says Greenbaum, "virtually all the money is put to work, not wasted on fat salaries, fancy offices and expensive cars."

His first significant investment, a year before the Access sale, was in KidSave International, an organization which rescues abandoned children warehoused in the former Soviet republics. KidSave subsequently became an unofficial partner in pursuing children's rights in Russia and providing help for 'graduates' of orphanages there. Later, Greenbaum moved into new areas, funding rescue centers in India and Togo for children enslaved in the sex trade, because needs there were far more serious than those in the former Soviet bloc.

He says "Business was easy. This stuff is hard."

His Foundation, with an approximate value today of $25 million, by law must disburse no less than 5% of the total each year, and he expects to add 10 to 20 million more in the next few years. Contributions so far amount to $3.7 million but venture philanthropy is only a part-time job. Divorced three times and currently single, Greenbaum is a full-time parent to four children - 5,7, 15 and 16 - a demanding, time-consuming job he takes seriously.

The part-time venture philanthropist feels his investments have all been satisfying, with no disappointments or misadventures, and says it's extremely unlikely he's been scammed since his projects have been "chosen well and responsibly." He emphasizes that his Foundation is about what can be done, not him, and consequently he is ambivalent about publicity. The Tribune interview was a first, attracting numerous requests for help which were politely turned down and three or four new contacts, including *The Happy Factory*, which promised to become "great projects."

"After Charlie emailed me in late October suggesting we get together in Salt Lake, I checked his Web site, decided *The Happy Factory* was not the type of organization I typically fund, and sent him a polite 'No thanks,'" says Greenbaum. "He emailed me back, explaining that he wasn't looking for funds but wanted to help me by supplying wooden toys to the needy children I identify."

The idea of getting instead of giving was so novel that he met with the Cooleys.

"Their passion and altruism were impressive. And their cost-effective operation, with volunteers doing all the work and no one taking a dime, does a tremendous amount of good. I loved everything they were doing and, when I learned about the new building fund, offered to match donations, dollar for dollar, up to $25,000," he explains.

That was for starters. When the Cooleys could only raise $18,000 in matching funds, Greenbaum kicked in $25,000 anyway. Then, when he discovered that people were neglecting their normal contributions to *The Happy Factory* in favor of the building fund, he quietly upped the ante with another $25,000 to help cover regular expenses.

He says "I generally don't get involved in domestic projects but I may become a regular contributor to their operation. I've decided that every community in the United States should have a *Happy Factory* and I want to give seed money to help create a national model."

Ed Kociela

A few of the Happy Factory's uncommon helpers

Steve Mills

Jim Greenbaum

Eric Lee

The Happy Factory - Ordinary people doing extraordinary things

Chapter 10 - Going international

The break-up of the Soviet Union in 1991 devastated member republics including Moldova.
Corruption was rampant in that ancient country, once part of Romania, where around 3% of the 4.4 million people are well-off and the remainder live in dire poverty. During the winter of 1998-1999, the Moldovan government estimated that 100 citizens were dying each week from lack of adequate food, heat, clothing and medical care.
In January of the following winter, Earl and Carolyn Snell arrived in Chisinau, the capital, on an LDS charities mission. After scrambling to find an apartment fit to live in, they went to work. Earl, a retired professor of business at Westminster College in Salt Lake City, began teaching Western business practices at the Technical University of Moldova with the aid of an interpreter, while Carolyn taught conversational English to his students and some of the faculty.
Their main mission, however, was to assess needs and get humanitarian aid into the country and, for this, they needed a Moldovan consignee to accept responsibility for the aid and clear it through Customs. Fortunately for all concerned, Ludmilla Scalnyi, wife of the University's vice rector and President of the Women's Organization of the Republic of Moldova, the umbrella for all the women's groups in the country, willingly took on that challenging job.
While the Snells waited for the first aid shipment to arrive, Ms Scalnyi, who was all too familiar with living conditions in Moldova's 10 districts, introduced them to the realities of life for most citizens with a visit to the village of Panachest. There, pensioners from the League of Retired Theater Veterans, all former producers, directors and theater and opera

stars, were left with nothing, trying to exist on 10 lei a month - about one U.S. dollar. Everyone in the village had become a farmer in their desperate fight for survival. To make matters even worse, the promised government support had been withdrawn from those who had been persuaded to adopt foster children, leaving some householders with as many as 10 'extra' children to feed and clothe.

. By the time the first aid shipment arrived five months late in May 1999, both Snells were impressed by their go-getting new friend Ludmilla Scalnyi.

Said Earl: "She had more connections than a Manhattan telephone directory and knew how to get things done."

As soon as Ms Scalnyi heard the shipment had reached Chisinau, she immediately swung into action and cleared the container through the labyrinthian Moldovan Customs red tape in two hours flat. This kind of speed was unheard of in any of the former Soviet republics where such imports could easily be held up for months and even a year.

In the container were clothes, school kits, games and wooden toys as well as badly-needed medical equipment. A delighted doctor in Chisinau said "Now we can do blood transfusions!" Medical scarcities were so severe that new babies were sent home wrapped in sheets of newspaper because neither his hospital nor the mother had anything better.

The Snells were surprised to find toys in the container and pleased by an invitation to attend Children's Day at the Republican Hospital, a stark and barren building in Chisinau. There, patients in the children's wing and their parents, all dressed in the best clothes they owned, were wide-eyed with wonder as the boxes from the United States were opened. Each child got clothes and a toy, and *The Happy Factory* cars and trucks were a special hit, with children driving them round and round the rim of a water-less fountain and pool.

"The children had never before had toys in the hospital and, although they were excited, it was the quietest excitement we'd ever seen. There was no pushing or shoving. Each child waited his or her turn," says Carolyn.

When the party was over, the children returned to their rooms and, on the way out of the hospital, Earl Snell entered one room to say goodbye. A couple of 4-year olds, playing with their new wooden cars, looked up at him almost with terror, so afraid that he wanted them back.

"We hadn't known toys were an option and, after the first shipment, we always ordered them," says Carolyn, adding that containers began to arrive regularly - 10 or 12 in the next 18 months - all with toys as well as food, clothes, medicine and books.

* * * * *

Dick and Arlene Outcalt opened *Happy Factory* #7 in Corvallis, Oregon, in October 1999.

Subsequently, Dick complained good-naturedly that when they delivered toys, they would leave them in a box at the front desk of a building or in someone's vehicle.

"We rarely got to see our *Happy Factory* toys 'in action,'" he says.

So when Arlene attended an International Home Economics conference in Accra, Ghana, in July 1999, he tagged along with a bag of 60 *Happy Factory* toys, hoping to see the fruits of their labor.

One of the hostesses at the conference graciously took the Outcalts and 30 of their toys to the OSU Children's Home in Accra.

"About 30 children were present and they all tried to reach in the bag at the same time, amid laughter and squeals, each one emerging with his or her own treasure. They were delighted and so were we," Dick says.

The Outcalts had treated themselves to a pre-conference visit to several African countries which included a game drive in Tanzania. They lugged along another 30 *Happy Factory* toys but ran out of time before they found a good place to leave them. When they boarded a small plane for their next stop in Zanzibar, only single seats were left. Dick ended up sitting beside Pedro Musigula, a Tanzanian government official, and they got to talking.

Asked about a needy orphanage, Pedro suggested one in his home town of Bukoba, in Tanzania's Kagera Region.

"We transferred all the toys right on the plane, from my bag to his," says Dick.

Later, the Outcalts were delighted to receive a letter from Pedro, thanking them again and explaining that the *Happy Factory* toys had been presented to the orphans of the non-governmental Umoja wa Maendeleo wa Wana-Minziro wa Bukoba in a brief ceremony on September 19th. He wrote in part:

"There are not any organizations foreseeing orphan problems in this area despite the fact that the number of orphans is increasing rapidly. They are very grateful for the gifts. They are making use of them and nowadays they are more active, friendly and jovial when playing with these toys."

* * * * *

Early in 2000, Harold Brown, Managing Director of LDS Welfare Services, was in Monrovia, Liberia, to observe delivery of humanitarian aid.

For a first-hand look at how well the aid was being disbursed in the country, founded in 1822 by freed black slaves from the United States and beset by military coups and civil war for more than 20 years, Brown ventured out of Monrovia to see how needs were being taken care of in the interior.

The trip took his party of four people to half a dozen villages. In each, the first order of business was to inquire about the basic food, clothing and other emergency needs of the children, and the need was great wherever they went. At one orphanage they visited, Brown reports the only toy was a soccer ball and the life-span of that ball was short because it was in constant use.

On several occasions, *Happy Factory* toys were handed out.

"I remember a tour we were given of another orphanage. Very poor. A compound of small huts with tin roofs and wall-to-wall children. Meals were cooked in one big pot, over an open fire. The children came up, one by one, and were given a wooden car or truck. For most of them, this was probably a first toy," says Brown.

Most children, shy and modest, couldn't suppress a smile and the words '*Happy Factory*' took on a new meaning. He adds that "One can hardly imagine a child without toys. It was a very rewarding moment. Those little toys really did spread happiness that day to 60 or 70 children."

* * * * *

A blank brain is not a condition normally associated with small children. Nor is it medically - or politically - correct to apply the term to an average child, no matter how disadvantaged. Yet it hints at the consequences, perhaps a bit exaggerated, when the brain of a child in the formative years, birth to age three, receives little or no stimulation. And this condition is what the ABCD program is designed to prevent.

The initials stand for A Basketful of Child Development, a program founded by veteran educators Drs. Ernie and Elaine Weeks, Ms Keith Elaine Packard and others in 1997, and tested initially on several dozen migrant families in 1998 in Brigham City, Utah, by Dr. Anne Austin.

The program operates on a fundamental principle that the first three years of life are the most critical for the development of a child's brain, a period in which mental and physical stimulation are vital. Parents, trained for at least 24 hours to be teachers, earn a Learning Basket of 18 commonplace materials such as a ball, doll, mirror, cup, colored straws and wooden blocks to help them stir the imagination and spur the learning ability of their children through interactive play.

Austin, a Utah State University professor, took a sabbatical half year in 1999 in Paraguay. There, in cooperation with the Peace Corps, she ran a pilot ABCD program in three small villages involving some 60 families. Learning Baskets, supplied by LDS Charities in Salt Lake City, came filled with a variety of things, including *Happy Factory* blocks, and had a remarkable impact.

Said one farmer "In the past, we went to the fields and worked, came home and went to bed. Now our minds have been awakened."

"As parents became involved and realized they could influence their children, their self-esteem rose," says Dr. Austin. She adds: "I encouraged the villagers to make their own Learning Baskets and collect the things that went into them. Initially, we had gorgeous hardwood blocks from the *Happy Factory*, all cut to scale."

Later, a village carpenter carefully duplicated them so well that Austin was moved to tears.

She explains that "Wooden blocks are an important part of a Learning Basket. They help the small and large motor development of small children as well as eye-hand coordination. For older kids, blocks are invaluable in learning counting, sorting, building and role playing."

In December 1999, Ernie and Elaine Weeks arrived in Port-au-Prince, Haiti, with 100 Learning Baskets on a special three month assignment as LDS Charities missionaries to implement the ABCD program and were impressed by the same kind of response Austin encountered in Paraguay.

For example, parents were separated into groups to experiment with the 750 wooden blocks supplied by *The Happy Factory* and think up new ways to use them.

"We were teaching them techniques for stimulating brains and were surprised at how rapidly they bloomed before our eyes," says Ernie Weeks.

"We found parents supportive once they grasped the concept of how they should interact with their child. We were warned that people would be tardy or wouldn't come at all but, in twelve sessions spread over three months, few were tardy and attendance was one hundred percent," adds his wife.

In March 2001, the Weeks arrived in Asuncion, Paraguay, to set up a three year ABCD program for 3,000 families suggested by Austin and funded by LDS Humanitarian Services. While awaiting governmental approval, five small ABCD projects were successfully completed. For example, in Abundancia, a village five hours drive from Asuncion, Elaine Weeks reports that "It changed the lives of the Nivacle women. They learned they could make a difference in the lives of their children. On our first visits, we had to wait for the mothers but, on our later visits, the mothers were waiting for us, Learning Baskets in hand."

Later that year, a telecast by an Asuncion TV station of an

ABCD session in a day care center aroused more interest in the power of Learning Baskets, and other day care centers in Paraguay began assembling their own baskets, including locally-made wooden blocks. In 2002, the main three year program got underway using 12,000 hardwood blocks from *The Happy Factory*. (See Chapter 9).

In the meantime, Dr. Austin's pilot program had been so successful that Pastoral del Nino (PDN), a Paraguayan Roman Catholic organization, wanted to introduce it nationwide with local people making and filling their own Learning Baskets.

Austin was enlisted as an Assessora and consultant and says "I spent two weeks in Paraguay in June 2003. In hinterland villages, people had turned milk bottles and pop bottles into toys and made dolls out of large gourds. Their imaginations had been awakened. It was so touching to see those home-made toys."

Testing of Pastoral's ABCD program has begun. What's needed, in addition to a nationwide ABCD program, are pre-schools for 4-5 year olds and a school-readiness program for children from 3 to 6. Since the future of any nation depends on its children, the idea is finally beginning to catch on in government circles. Fortunately, in a country where church and state are closely entwined, the Roman Catholic Church is a strong supporter of those first educational baskets and *Happy Factory* building blocks.

* * * * *

Children are children the world over where a toy is concerned. No cultural blocks, no language barrier. Just ask Devin Griner, a second year medical student at the University of Utah who has been involved with Operation Smile since he was in high school nine years before.

Operation Smile, headquartered in Norfolk, Virginia, is an international organization of doctors and nurses who travel to Third World countries in teams to repair cleft palates, cleft lips, club feet, severe burn damage and other medical problems. Team members donate their time, pay their own way and offer their expertise free of charge.

Griner's interest was first aroused in 1994 when his father, a TV cameraman, was part of a crew which produced a documentary film of an Operation Smile team at work in China called 'Faces of Hope.'

"That was what led me to med school. I was blown away by what the doctors did. I decided I wanted to be a reconstructive plastic surgeon," says Griner, explaining that repairing a cleft lip is usually a relatively simple, 30-minute procedure involving cutting through three layers of tissue and muscle and stitching the pieces together.

He started an Operation Smile club at his high school and, the next year, was a junior member of a medical team that spent two weeks in Danang, Vietnam. A typical team consists of a leader, six or seven plastic surgeons, six or seven anesthesiologists, a pediatrician, a dentist or orthodontist, twelve nurses, a bio-med technician, a Child Life chief therapist and assistant therapist, two medical record keepers plus a couple of dozen in-country helpers including interpreters/ translators, usually from local schools. Two week trips have proven the most effective. The medical teams work 16 hour days and have only one day to sight-see.

"Danang was the biggest shock of my life. We encountered kids with every misfortune you could imagine," says Griner, whose job was to help relax children before surgery and make presentations on oral hygiene and nutrition at local schools. The Operation Smile team could only operate on one-third of the children they screened and turning the others away was the toughest part of the trip.

In August 2002, high school students at Utah's Operation Smile clubs organized the week-long Operation Smile international conference held at the University of Utah and decided the 500 attendees should paint *Happy Factory* cars and truck. The Cooleys supplied 500 and, two months later, Griner took time off from school, stuffed 200 of them in a back pack and joined a 35 member Operation Smile team that flew to Beijing and Chonqing, then bused the last lap to Du Jian Yan city, in China's Szechuan province.

Two days of screening were followed by five days operating

on 160 people ranging from little children to the elderly, with cleft lips on adults done on an out-patient basis.

"A half hour operation can make a dramatic change in a person's life," says Griner.

By this time, he had trained as a medical record keeper and, wearing his back pack on his daily rounds, gave a toy to each child as he or she came out of anesthesia. Their reaction varied. For many, it was their first toy and they were dumbfounded.

"The parents were excited by the gifts and, when told U.S. students had painted the toys, became quite emotional. They were amazed that foreigners would take the time to do such a thing," explains Griner, adding that "The Chinese are some of the most appreciative people I've ever met. They were so grateful for what had been done for their children that they got down on their knees, crying so hard that the pant legs of our doctors were soaked with tears."

Operation Smile teams can handle only a fraction of those with cleft lips and cleft palates so, during their two weeks in-country, they teach local doctors how to do the job. And the spirit of volunteerism is spreading, with Filipino and other foreign doctors, for example, joining Operation Smile teams.

* * * * *

An adventure in Romania began with a telephone call to the Cooleys early in 2003 from Pam Snow, wife, mother and airline employee in Cedar.

Pam, her three sisters and her two sisters-in-law were planning a trip to Bucharest where her parents, Pat and Joan Richan, were on an 18 month humanitarian mission. They decided to take along whatever they could for needy children, including *Happy Factory* toys, and the Cooleys ended up as co-conspirators of a special kind.

The six women, warned in advance by the Richans about the incredible difficulty of getting anything past Romanian Customs officials, were nervous. They had collected 172 blankets, 107 dolls, 30 stuffed bears, a portable basketball stand, a stick horse, crib mobiles, baby toys, play dough, 50 fleece hats, two jackets, 90 pairs of socks, 54 underwear, slippers, sleepers, 150 bags of candy and $2,000 in cash donated by friends and neighbors.

"We packed and re-packed but couldn't find room for the two *Happy Factory* steam shovels anywhere but in their fitted cartons," Pam explains, so they filled the empty spaces around the shovels with 200 *Happy Factory* cars and trucks and crossed their fingers.

A request to the airlines for an extra weight allowance was granted and, when they met in the Phoenix, Arizona, airport terminal on March 17, 2003, the travelers checked in 22 suitcases and the two large *Happy Factory* steam shovel cartons before climbing aboard with their backpacks. On arrival in Bucharest the next afternoon, they decided to pick up their luggage separately, each with a cart.

"We wished each other luck and I took one steam shovel and my sister Lynette took the other. We put each on the bottoms of a cart and piled the rest of the luggage on top," says Pam

Immigration officers looked at their passports. There were no Customs declarations to be filled out and Customs officers asked what was in their luggage.

"Toys," said Pam.

"Okay," an officer replied, waving her through without further ado.

The other five breezed through with equal ease and the Richans couldn't believe what had happened..

A dilapidated van with bald tires delivered the visitors to the Hotel Manuc. The next morning, after a sound sleep, they were off by taxi to St. Maria's Placement Center, the new, politically-correct name of an orphanage, in a tough section of Bucharest, with clothes, candy, wooden cars, a steam shovel and a bag of plastic balls to use with the shovel.

"Excited three and four year olds jumped into our arms, talking in Romanian and grabbing for the cars. There were only two attendants to look after 35 children, with little time for tender loving care," reports Pam.

Upstairs, 9 and 10 year olds in two classrooms were given candy. Asked to say something in English, they chorused "My shoes are dirty but I cleaned them for you!"

The next day they were introduced to Micki and her mother, educated gypsies who ran St. Nicholas, a non-government school for children in 50 gypsy families. The visitors spent some of the $2,000 to fill 50 bags with groceries which they delivered to Micki's office. The families filed in for the food and each of their children chose a fleece hat, blanket and toy.

"A 13-year old boy picked a red truck which our interpreter explained had been painted by my 13-year old daughter and it was just a neat experience," says Pam.

Later, without advance notice, they stopped at a children hospital and, after an hour of negotiating, were allowed in.

"It was shocking. We visited six rooms, each with eight children and their parents who were there to look after them," Pam explains.

The toy cars, dolls, and hats were unloaded from backpacks and passed out with much pleasure for the givers as well as the receivers.

A highlight of the trip was a 7-hour train ride to Timisuara in northern Romania to visit Onesimus Brothers, a Baptist-run home for boys 4 to 21 years old. The Director and 21 boys met the visitors at a shopping mall where each boy picked out a pair of new shoes and socks purchased with some more of the donated money. Back at the home, each boy was given candy, a hat and a toy car, and the second steam shovel was delivered.

"One little boy stood and thanked us and they all sang a song. Another boy stood and thanked us and they sang another song. This was the cherry on the top of the trip. You could see this visit making a difference in the lives of those boys," says Pam.

She adds that, during their 10 days in Romania, "We passed out *Happy Factory* toys to gypsy children in the street, children in stores and in the subway, just wherever we saw a child. We knew that even the children not in 'placement centers' would still enjoy having a toy. Most came from pretty humble circumstances. And the toys never seemed to end. We'd put 30 in a backpack and draw from it all day and still have extra. It was truly the 'loaves and the fishes.'"

* * * * *

Karen Croft, a veteran Operating Room nurse, has accompanied no less than 15 Operation Smile teams in a five year period, contributing her skills to the underprivileged in Brazil, Colombia, India, Kenya, Peru, Venezuela, Vietnam and other countries.

She explains that "In all these countries, there are the rich and the poor and no welfare. We operate on people who cannot afford medical care."

A typical trip took her to Belhorizante, Brazil, on Wednesday, August 19th, 2003, at the end of a lengthy airplane ride from Salt Lake City via Miami and Sao Paulo. After checking into the Life Center Hotel, adjacent to the Life Center Hospital, the tired team of visitors spent the afternoon talking with local colleagues about what they would need for the 11 day medical marathon that lay ahead.

Surgery had to be within the scope of the team's equipment and supplies, and the next two days, spent screening some 400 candidates, ended with the difficult job of selecting the 130 most suitable for an operation, most of them children.

"Screening is a really tense time for parents and their children. Everything looks and smells so different and the children are scared to death. We gave each of them a toy to help alleviate their anxiety and quiet them down," explains Croft.

She and a colleague had each brought 150 *Happy Factory* cars and trucks and she reports that, when they opened their bags so the children could pick what they wanted, the girls always chose a pink car. She adds that "They loved *The Happy Factory* cars and trucks. Some had never had a toy before and were fearful that we might take them back."

Preparing for surgery took most of Saturday and, on Sunday, the team took a sightseeing trip by bus into the mountains to re-charge their batteries and be ready for surgery week. From Monday to Friday, in a demanding schedule that began every morning at 7AM and ended sometime between 8 PM and 10 PM that night, the visiting professionals completed 130 operations.

"It was exhausting but you got an adrenaline rush because

what you were doing felt so good," says Croft. "Surgeons who may be demanding or difficult at home helped unpack supplies and worked with whatever was available without having a fit. They were just princes in the operating rooms. Their human decency was unmatched."

* * * * *

In September 2003, 100 *Happy Factory* cars and trucks played a star role in a strange Bulgarian orphanage procedure of 'now you see them, now you don't.'

The toy vehicles had arrived in the baggage of Kelly Anderson of Spanish Fork, Utah, along with a *Happy Factory* steam shovel, medicines, educational supplies and two baby swings. She and her two partners in One Heart, a non-profit organization formed earlier that year to aid orphans in Bulgaria, were following up with a two week swing to assess needs in the Balkan Republic on the Black Sea where communism was revoked by parliament in 1990.

Anderson, Glyn Barker and Deborah Gardner were Mormon missionaries in the Montana-sized country of 8 million in 1994-95 and found poverty and privation still all too common, especially for orphans who were routinely warehoused and neglected during the communist era. The initial groundwork had already been laid after Barker assisted a friend with a baby adoption in 1999 and began fund-raising to supplement the food budgets of a few orphanages.

During the September visit, nine orphanages scattered around the country were identified as prime targets, a One Heart office was opened in Sofia, a director and six part-time staffers were hired, a car was purchased and regular help was scheduled. With funding from 14 sponsoring groups in the U.S., fresh produce and food is delivered weekly to the orphanages, the car is available as an ambulance when and where needed, and an Interaction Resource Center established in Sofia supplies books, cassettes, videos, musical instruments and toys which One Heart staffers take to orphanages on regular visits - and bring back to the center.

They found the orphanages old, dirty and ill-maintained, with broken windows, dormitories holding tattered mattresses, and little furniture or furnishings. Life for the inmates was primitive at best. Each morning, children dipped into bins for the 'unisex' clothing they would wear that day. In one orphanage, there were three pieces of Lego for 200 children to share. In another, a 12 year old girl had pasted to the wall a picture of a shampoo bottle she wanted.

"Everything was communal. The children were allowed to play with the *Happy Factory* toys but could not own them. That's the Bulgarian system," Kelly explains.

The *Happy Factory* steam shovel donated by the Cooleys now occupies a special place in an orphanage for children with physical and mental disabilities where it's both a toy and an invaluable learning tool.

"I thought babies would be the most heart-wrenching children but it was the teenagers, ostracized in school, with no chance of adoption, no future and no hope," says Kelly.

Most workers in Bulgarian orphanages get little training and their jobs are considered menial so One Heart is partnering with a local foundation to develop a training program for them involving weekly classes.

In August 2004, since the things brought the previous September did not stretch nearly far enough, One Heart shipped a 40 foot container to Bulgaria. It was filled with food, clothes, shoes, quilts, 3,000 blankets, medicines, hygiene items, educational kits, art supplies, 400 *Happy Factory* toys, six *Happy Factory* steam shovels plus breathing machines, walkers, crutches and other equipment for the physically handicapped.

"The first container was a learning experience for us and for them and we plan to provide many more, one each year," says Kelly. "And we'd like the children to have the pleasure of owning their own *Happy Factory* toy. Children in orphanages for 7 to 18 year olds have lockers and maybe the Bulgarian system can be changed a little."

Miles of smiles around the world - in China ...

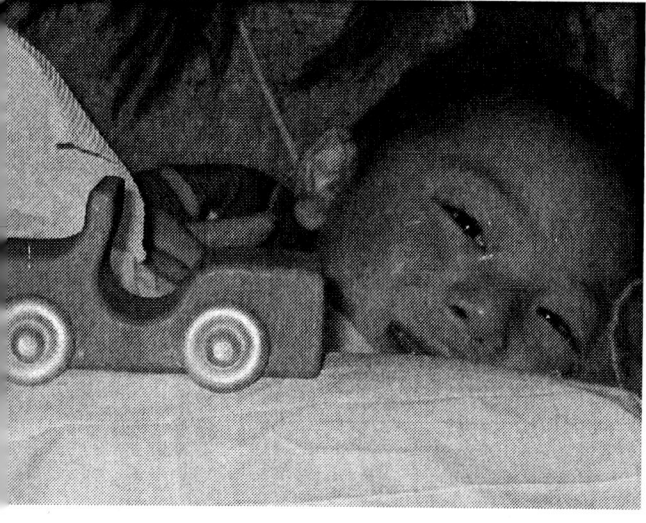

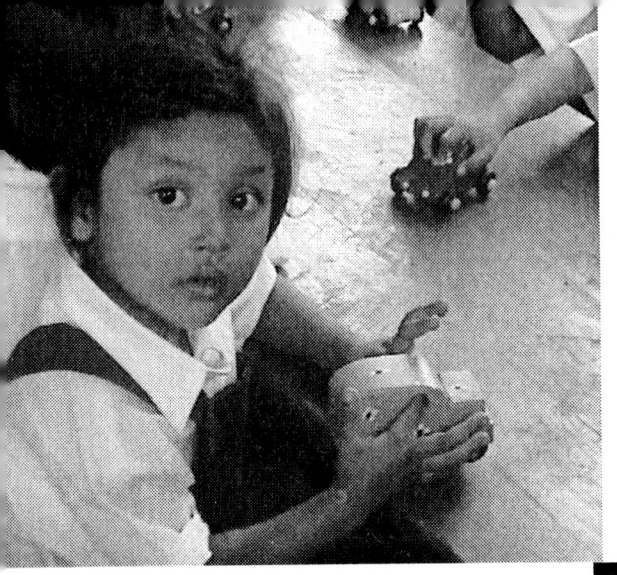

Nicaragua

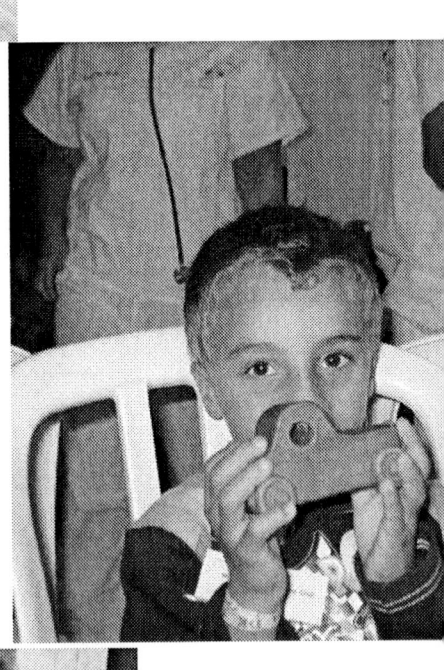

and Brazil...

 Romania,

 Liberia

 and Ghana

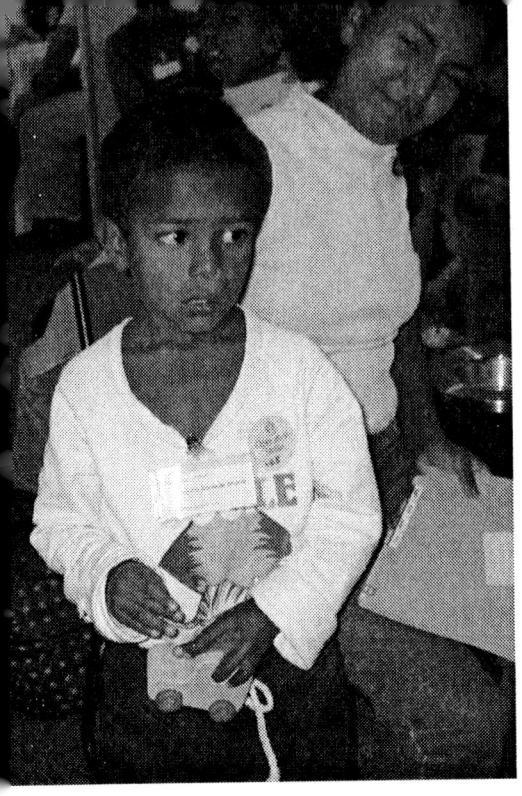

although enthusiasm is not unanimous.

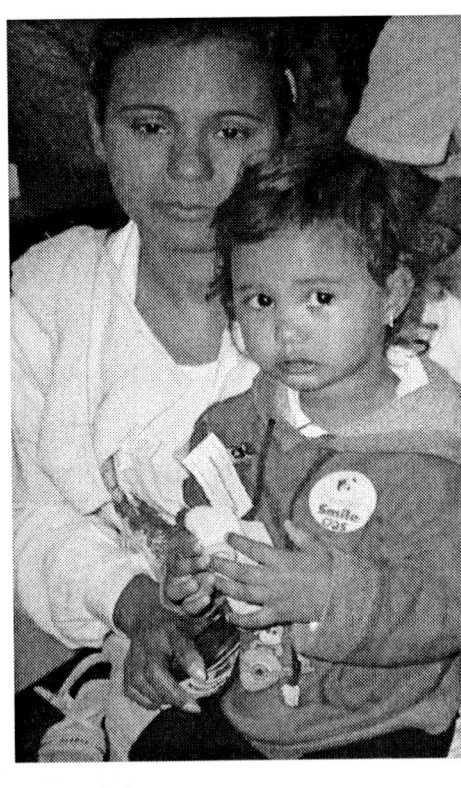

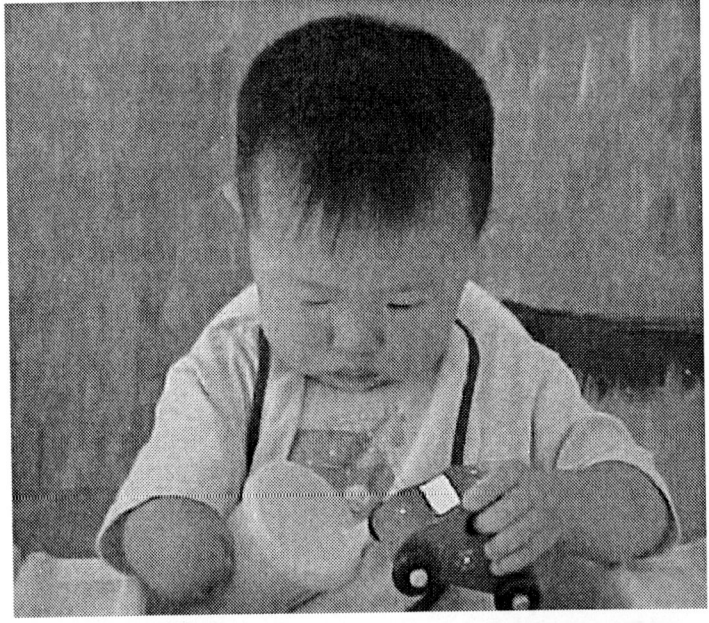

The Happy Factory - Ordinary people doing extraordinary things

Chapter 11 - What's next?

Thursday, March 25th, 2004, was a big day in the life of *The Happy Factory*, marking the start of succession, a change of command and a move into new quarters.

The idea of moving production from the Metalcraft Technologies building was never even a random thought for the Cooleys until operating hours there unexpectedly changed. The original agreement was ideal. David Grant was a generous and genial landlord and *The Happy Factory* was a prized tenant, able to operate rent-free whenever and however the Cooleys pleased.

Then Metalcraft, which had been operating from 5 AM until midnight, five days a week, was buffeted by the fallout from a U.S. economic downturn. Orders began to shrink and early in November 2002 Grant was forced to eliminate Metalcraft's swing shift. Because much of the company's business was with the U.S. military, security measures were strictly enforced. With the building locked up tight at 5 PM, it was no longer possible for *The Happy Factory* to operate in the evening or continue to host groups "after hours."

"At first, we thought 'Yippee! No more evening work.' But when I informed Scoutmaster Lansing Ellsworth that we would have to cancel his troop's Thursday night work session on various projects outlined in the Boy Scout manual, he was upset," explained Charles.

"That's not fair. I can't teach my boys in a basketball arena," said Scoutmaster Ellsworth, referring to the recreation room in their LDS Ward chapel where they held their regular meetings. "You need to build your own building."

"Well, that takes a lot of money," Charles replied.

Scoutmaster Ellsworth was unimpressed. "So what? There's

The Happy Factory

lots of money out there for a good cause and *The Happy Factory* is one of the best."

That brief conversation was a catalyst, producing a fresh perspective. All of a sudden, instead of rejoicing about shorter hours, Charles and Donna felt badly about not being able to accommodate evening activities anymore. This got them to thinking harder and harder about alternatives as autumn turned to winter and Mother Nature brightened Cedar City neighborhoods with a carpet of snow and delivered a white Christmas.

"Some people say they don't mind progress as long as it doesn't change anything, and that's about the way we felt," explains Charles. "But progress had overtaken *The Happy Factory*. We'd been growing and growing fast. By the end of that year, 21 *Happy Factories* were in operation and more than 220,000 *Happy Factory* toys had been delivered to needy children all over the world."

At the Board of Trustees meeting in January 2003, Charles related his conversation with Scoutmaster Ellsworth and said "It would appear that *The Happy Factory* has been overtaken by progress and will have to change."

The eight Board members present stroked their chins (there wasn't a beard in the bunch) and pondered the implications of his remark. In a few minutes, they decided unanimously that, due to circumstances way beyond their control, not only *The Happy Factory* but Cedar was in need of a building dedicated exclusively to community projects of one kind and another as well as toy production.

Individual Board members called several other prominent members of the community and found it required little effort or argument to enlist these involuntary volunteers in a Fund Raising Committee. At the first committee meeting at noon on March 10th in Mark Kohler's law office, Charles explained that he had made some rough drawings of a floor plan and shown them to Connel Gower, a general contractor and developer.

"Connel estimated $128,000 for the building and said if we built it in his Coal Creek Industrial Park he'd give us $10,000 off the price of the lot. With that incentive, the new committee was quickly organized and agreed that the project was commendable, funding was feasible and the ball started rolling," says Charles.

Fund raising got underway and was high-lighted by a benefit gala dinner August 14th in Cedar, attended by 384 people with Thurl Bailey as Master of Ceremonies, which raised almost $28,000 as mentioned in the previous chapter. Other private donations totaled $18,000 and were matched and topped off by the James R. Greenbaum Foundation to the tune of $25,000.

Ground breaking on September 23, 2003, was handled expertly by two young cousins, Austin Palmer, 5, and Dustin Palmer, 5, aboard two *Happy Factory* steam shovels.

"The boys were chosen because Kristine knew them and knew they could be excused from school that morning," says Charles with a grin.

To avoid any possible conflict of interest so that builders and suppliers would be free to donate whatever they could, Connel Gower excused himself from construction of the new *Happy Factory*. XL Builders of Cedar, chosen as the General Contractor, enlisted several subcontractors including Premier Heating, Jones Plumbing and Zion Plumbing, Total Electric and CED Electric. In what amounted to a typical labor of love for *The Happy Factory*, subcontractors as well as suppliers such as Anderson Lumber donated material or time or both. Paul Cozzens supplied cupboards and the elaborate piping and exhaust system that collects and removes dust, and Rainbow Sign and Banner created and donated the elaborate sign that graces the front of the building.

"We had more fun making that sign. Everyone got involved and excited about it," says Jeff Dansie, the company owner.

"The appraised value of the new *Happy Factory* is $161,200 compared to our cost of $126,723.16. The difference was donated time and material," explains a delighted Charles Cooley.

The new 40 foot by 80 foot, pre-engineered steel-truss metal building, white with green trim, designed by Charles, was completed March 19, 2004 and sits proudly one story high just off Airport Road one-half mile north of Utah Route 56 about one mile northwest of the previous location in the Metalcraft building.

Volunteers began hauling everything moveable out of the old quarters into the new building almost immediately and the Grand Opening on March 25th was followed by a come one, come all Open House on March 26th and 27th.

At the Grand Opening, Charles Cooley said "What's so remarkable to Donna and me is that we started out making toys for needy children but we don't do that anymore. We found out that *Happy Factory* toys are tools for the mind and, in the process, we help rejuvenate minds."

Another speaker was Garry Flake, Director of Humanitarian Emergency Services for the Church of Jesus Christ of Latter-Day Saints. Flake spoke without notes but the gist of his remarks was simple and memorable. 'LDS Emergency Services has dealt with more than 180 countries in distress. I have visited half of them and personally witnessed about every terrible condition in which a child can live. Many times I have been present when a *Happy Factory* toy has been put in the hands of a child. I have seen them hug these small gifts and knew that often this was the first toy that child had ever owned. Because of my first-hand experiences like these, I feel qualified to represent the children of the world and to thank *The Happy Factory* on their behalf.'

In the new *Happy Factory*, which is twice the size of previous quarters, volunteers are able to do everything they did in the old one and then some, day or night, week in week out, all year round. In addition to spacious housing for toy making machinery and equipment, there is a 1,000 square foot room with tables, chairs, two state-of-the-art sewing machines, a serger, four quilting frames, a DVD/Video player and catalogs of humanitarian and Eagle Scout projects which include all the necessary guidelines and instructions.

"It's a first class facility that can accommodate up to fifty people for service projects. To date we have had Eagle Scouts, Sons of the Utah Pioneers, Relief Society groups, young men and women groups and Southern Utah University groups numbering from 12 to 65 participants in evening projects and several more are scheduled to begin," says Charles.

Operating the new, free-standing *Happy Factory* in 2004 cost $44,500 and $58,000 is budgeted for 2005. This compares with the cost-free tenancy at Metalcraft Technologies. Yet the savings only hint at the true value of David Grant's support for the past five years. While he regrets losing his prized tenant, Grant is an enthusiastic fan of the move forward.

"It's been fun to watch *The Happy Factory* evolve. We will miss them but it's progress. The new building will be an important part of the succession process," says Grant.

Quietly and unofficially, Grant has offered guidance and counsel on several occasions. In a wide-ranging conversation with Charles in February 2003, amid the initial planning for the new building, he asked politely but bluntly: "Do you and Donna want *The Happy Factory* to continue operating after you're gone?"

He went on to explain that *"The Happy Factory's* long-term future will depend on your succession plan. There are good people on the Board of Trustees but there will be a metamorphosis. You and Donna are founders, with different traits and commitments than those who will take over when you can no longer manage things. Most charitable organizations have to pay their managers and fund raisers. Raising money for *The Happy Factory* so far has been easier since no one is paid and every dollar goes for product. As an organization, *The Happy Factory's* future is still uncertain, but the concept is so magical that someone is bound to step up."

Fortunately for everyone concerned, someone has.

The conversation with Grant was another catalyst that got Charles and Donna pondering questions they had not seriously considered before. The biggest of all was the easiest to answer - yes, both agreed, they wanted *The Happy Factory* to continue operating and to grow. Yet deciding exactly how to make that happen was more difficult.

At a series of monthly family meetings that followed the February talk with David Grant, rough ideas about the future shape of *The Happy Factory* were smoothed into shape. All four Cooleys recognized that more help would be needed to manage and operate the new building with its extended operating hours. Nominally, the *Happy Factory* would be open for volunteer toy makers Monday through Friday from 9 AM until 5 PM, year 'round. In addition, it would be available for groups and organizations, by appointment only, on Tuesday, Wednesday and Thursday evenings from 5 PM until 9 PM.

"As we saw it, the new organization would have to be made up of a number of people with small responsibilities rather than a few people with large responsibilities," says Charles

"The new facility opened up many new positions we weren't aware we needed before, such as schedulers, shift supervisors, production inspectors, shippers, accountants and office managers. We'd done it all before. Now the chores would be shared," adds Donna.

At the same time, the familiar old routine and ground rules remain unchanged. No one earns a dime. All the work is done by volunteers who come when they can, do what they want, and leave when they want to. And newcomers are always welcome.

One example: when the telephone rang in the Cooley home one evening. a retired Certified Public Accountant identified himself and said "I'm no good at making toys but I'd be happy to help you keep the books."

Neither daughter wished to take over from their parents as managers and much thought was given to who should succeed Charles as President and Chief Executive Officer.

"During the fund-raising campaign, Mark Kohler, the Chairman of our Board, showed outstanding leadership and a sincere desire to benefit *The Happy Factory*. When I approached him with the suggestion that he become President and Chief Executive Officer, he was very humble, even teary-eyed," says Charles.

"The funding project was divinely controlled," Mark adds modestly. "Everything fell into place and, as expected, most of the money came from Cedar sources. From small means great things come about."

Everyone agrees that Charles and Donna Cooley are

irreplaceable and will remain deeply involved in *Happy Factory* matters - and that Kohler, 36, is uniquely qualified to take command.

Mark was born and raised in Salt Lake City, got a Bachelor's of Science degree in accounting in 1996 and a Master's in taxation accounting in 1997 from the University of Utah, and a Juris Doctor from the Williamette University College of Law in Salem, Oregon, in 2000. He is a Certified Public Accountant as well as an attorney with Marchant, Kohler & Kyler, a Cedar law firm, and specializes in business, estate and tax planning. He is married with three children and enjoys a variety of sports including golf and skiing.

At a meeting on March 25th, 2004, before the official Grand Opening of the new building, the Board of Trustees unanimously approved the restructuring of *The Happy Factory* and Mark's confirmation as the new President and CEO.

"Mark Kohler is exactly the right one to succeed me," Charles says emphatically.

To make sure he will have enough time for his new, unpaid duties as head of the *Happy Factory*, the hard-working lawyer resigned from the Cedar Rotary Club and Chamber of Commerce. Sitting at his desk in his shirt-sleeves, despite a towering stack of caseload folders on the shelf behind him, Mark is obviously comfortable with his new responsibilities yet well aware of the fresh challenges ahead.

He says: "The new and bigger *Happy Factory* will be great for the needy children of the world and expanded operations beyond Utah will make legal planning, accounting, tax reporting and managerial operations more critical. The legal complexities of *Happy Factory* operations are growing exponentially. For example, the liability exposure is different in different States. New licensing, registration and insurance issues for a non-profit organization have to be addressed. At the federal level, IRS compliance is becoming more daunting and we must make sure that members of the Board and Happy Factors are not personally liable."

Since it's far more than a one man job and Mark can only spread himself so thin, he plans to deputize and delegate as much as possible to *Happy Factory* Trustees and others.

For the present at least, Donna Cooley has agreed to remain as Secretary-Treasurer, assisted with financial matters by Trustee Paul Cozzens. Jolene Cooley Lee remains as Vice President, responsible for handling volunteers and tours of the new facility. Kristine Cooley continues in charge of policies and procedures pertaining to the growing number of *Happy Factory* branches. To lighten the load on the new president, other Trustees will have specific responsibilities. Thurl Bailey, for example, is in charge of the annual fund raising galas while Jon Absey handles promotion

That said, you can be sure that Charles and Donna Cooley will remain immersed up to their ears or even higher in *Happy Factory* activities large and small. The amazing organization they founded has become the focus of their lives and will undoubtedly remain so, but life for both of them should be a bit easier as others share more of the burden.

Says Charles. "Part of the time, we will be unofficial *Happy Factory* Ambassadors, doing whatever needs to be done wherever that may take us."

The scope of their new duties as Ambassadors, unofficial or official, has not yet been clearly defined and will, of course, be in addition to showing up for work almost every day at the new *Happy Factory* and making regular deliveries and business trips to Salt Lake City.

Equally unclear is the precise course *The Happy Factory* will take in the future.

"Neither the Cooleys nor I are interested in growing rapidly. Charles and Donna had no plans for growth. *The Happy Factory* grew naturally in the past and will do so in the future. We're only at the tip of the iceberg and don't know what's underneath. But the opportunities are great. Rotary and Lions clubs, prisons, Senior Citizens centers - a *Happy Factory* can fit in anywhere," says Mark.

"An easy, inexpensive way to expand would be into mobile home parks in Arizona, southern California, Texas and Florida. They provide parking pads for the 'snow birds' who flee south every winter to spend four or five months in the sun and soon run out of things to do," adds Charles. He explains that such parks usually include a woodworking shop which could easily become a *Happy Factory* and says "Time is the most precious thing people have and look how many people waste it. Mel Griguhn said the other day 'Thank goodness for the *Happy Factory*.'"

Another possibility Charles and Mark foresee are community-backed centers, similar to the new *Happy Factory* in Cedar City, suitable for service projects of all kinds as well as toy making.

"I see *The Happy Factory* growing slowly but surely. We will help some of the current branches expand and test service possibilities in their community, and we will welcome the addition of new factories wherever someone decides there's a need," says Mark. The fact that *The Happy Factory* is a 100% volunteer organization he considers both a handicap and a blessing. "It would be great to have salaried management but we don't want paid staff. That would put limitations on our growth."

Unsurprisingly, Kohler and the Cooleys are on the same wave length and in agreement on everything that matters most.

Says Charles "We've thought a lot about the future of *The Happy Factory*. We've created the structure for a perpetual *Happy Factory*. We're geared to last forever."

Mark Kohler, Happy Factory President

Charles and Donna Cooley
Founders and Ambassadors of Goodwill

The Happy Factory - Ordinary people doing extraordinary things

Epilogue

Charles Cooley is entitled to a few last words in this story about *The Happy Factory*.

With appropriate apologies to Sir Winston Churchill, he says "This isn't the end. This isn't even the beginning of the end. This is only the end of the beginning."

And Mark Kohler adds that "There may be different kinds of Happy Factories in the future, ranging from garages to service centers, but the objective will always be the same - anyone who wants to serve needy children can do so."

The Happy Factory Inc. Web site is www.happyfactory.org.

For those wanting more information, Mark or Charles can be reached at World Headquarters by mail at 896 North 2175 West Circle, Cedar City, Utah 84720, by phone (435) 586 8352, by FAX (435) 586 2294 or by email happy@infowest.com.

All royalties from sales of this book will go to *The Happy Factory*. Those wishing to purchase additional copies of the book can contact Happy Factory World Headquarters, major booksellers such as Barnes & Noble and Border's, or log onto Amazon.com and type the name of the book and/or the author's name in the Search window.

Printed in the United States
40448LVS00009B/223-243